A GOLDEN VOICE

TED WILLIAMS

A GOLDEN VOICE

How Faith, Hard Work, and Humility
Brought Me from the Streets
to Salvation

WITH BRET WITTER

GOTHAM BOOKS

GOTHAM BOOKS
Published by Penguin Group (USA) Inc.
375 Hudson Street, New York, New York 10014, U.S.A.
Penguin Group (Canada), 90 Eglinton Avenue East, Suite 700, Toronto, Ontario M4P
2Y3, Canada (a division of Pearson Penguin Canada Inc.); Penguin Books Ltd, 80 Strand,
London WC2R 0RL, England; Penguin Ireland, 25 St Stephen's Green, Dublin 2, Ireland (a
division of Penguin Books Ltd); Penguin Group (Australia), 250 Camberwell Road, Cam-
berwell, Victoria 3124, Australia (a division of Pearson Australia Group Pty Ltd); Penguin
Books India Pvt Ltd, 11 Community Centre, Panchsheel Park, New Delhi—110 017, India;
Penguin Group (NZ), 67 Apollo Drive, Rosedale, Auckland 0632, New Zealand (a division
of Pearson New Zealand Ltd); Penguin Books (South Africa) (Pty) Ltd, 24 Sturdee Avenue,
Rosebank, Johannesburg 2196, South Africa

Penguin Books Ltd, Registered Offices: 80 Strand, London WC2R 0RL, England

Published by Gotham Books, a member of Penguin Group (USA) Inc.

First printing, May 2012
10   9   8   7   6   5   4   3   2   1

PHOTO CREDITS
All insert photos courtesy of Julia Williams, except for page 5 bottom, courtesy of public do-
main; page 6 top and middle, courtesy of Colleen Sariotis; page 6 bottom, courtesy of Gus
Sariotis; page 7, courtesy of Doral Chenoweth; page 8 top, courtesy of Melissa Killian; page
8 middle, courtesy of Bret Adams; and page 8 bottom, courtesy of Gus Sariotis.

Gotham Books and the skyscraper logo are trademarks of Penguin Group (USA) Inc.

LIBRARY OF CONGRESS CATALOGING-IN-PUBLICATION DATA
Williams, Ted, 1957–
A golden voice : how faith, hard work and humility brought me from the streets to salvation /
Ted Williams; with Bret Witter.
p. cm.
ISBN 978-1-592-40714-9 (hbk.)
1. Williams, Ted, 1957– 2. African Americans—Biography. 3. African American homeless
persons—Biography. 4. Addicts—Rehabilitation—United States. 5. Television announcing.
6. Radio announcing. I. Witter, Bret. II. Title.
E185.97.W734A3 2012
973.92092—dc23
[B]
2011050998

Printed in the United States of America
Set in Minister and Gotham
Designed by Chris Welch

While the author has made every effort to provide accurate telephone numbers and Internet
addresses at the time of publication, neither the publisher nor the author assumes any
responsibility for errors, or for changes that occur after publication. Further, the publisher
does not have any control over and does not assume any responsibility for author or third-
party Web sites or their content.

Penguin is committed to publishing works of quality and integrity.
In that spirit, we are proud to offer this book to our readers;
however, the story and the experiences are Ted and Kathy's alone.

Some names have been changed to protect the privacy of the individuals involved.

To God,
my savior, who has blessed me,
and
to Kathy, for sticking with me, and
Momma, for never losing faith

PROLOGUE

It's hard for me to watch the famous minute-long clip on YouTube, the one of me standing on the street corner with my little cardboard sign. The world might hear a homeless man with a golden voice saying, "When you're listening to nothing but the best of oldies, you're listening to Magic 98.9," but I see a version of myself I don't like: crazy hair sticking out in all directions, unshaven, brown rotten teeth, dirty camouflage jacket. I see the desperate eyes of a hustler out of hustles, an addict at the end of two decades of bad decisions with nothing left to do but smile and perform for a guy who rolls down his window and says those famous nine words: "I'm going to make you work for your dollar."

I'm embarrassed. I really am. Because that video is no lie. That was my life. Back in the day, I used to be somebody—a husband, a father, a successful radio personality. Then, on August 20, 1988, I smoked crack cocaine, and over a period of two months it took hold of me until I was smoking cat litter off my filthy floors because I thought it might be crack, and selling my son's baby clothes for drugs. I lost everything: my job, my home, my children, my morals, my self-respect; and for almost twenty years, right up until the morning I appeared on the *Today* show in January 2011, I was a homeless addict.

This is not a pretty book, because homelessness and addiction are not a pretty life. The things I've done and the places I've been might send shivers down your spine. I laid up in grimy crack houses. I robbed my prostitute girlfriend's clients in seedy motels. I carried my clothes in a plastic bag and went weeks without a shower. I conned my poor momma. I stole from my only friends. I slept for three days in a nest of spiders at the bottom of a concrete staircase, comatose on crack, and walked around with holes in my shoes so bad the snow came in and peeled the flesh off the bottom of my feet. I kept a mental list of every store I'd stolen from and which clerk was working at the time, because over a period of decades, in an endless desperate hustle for drug money, I burned the retail sector of Columbus, Ohio, to the ground. And I smoked crack cocaine with every last cent.

I ate my grandson's baby food, even though I knew my daughter couldn't afford more. I smoked the money my mother sent me to attend my father's funeral, then had the nerve to call long-distance on the day they put him in the ground and ask for more. I lived in condemned buildings, abandoned restaurants, and once, for several months, under a tent I made out of children's raincoats. I crapped in buckets. I ate pizza off the ground. I cursed men and used women and once, God help me, broke my girlfriend Kathy's arm in three places with one unfortunate slap.

You're not going to like me for some of this book. I'm going to tell you that now. There will be times when you want to turn away. Everybody else did. My momma. My children. My ex-wife. The social workers, the do-gooders, the drug counselors. Heck, I even turned away from my own life. I fell into a hopeless state of mind and soul, because I was an addict and my life had shrunk to the point that it was nothing but crack—and who would want to look at that?

Only Kathy, a fellow addict, stayed with me.

Only Kathy . . . and God. He was always talking to me, always trying to send me down the right path. I thought the voice was in my head, and I didn't want to hear it. I didn't want to acknowledge Him, because I knew I was doing wrong and I didn't think I had the strength to do right. Finally, when I reached the end of my chain, I listened. Not half listened, telling myself, "It's okay to do what you're doing, Ted, you're still a Christian," but really listened. Really acknowledged God in my heart.

And what did He do? He put me on the street corner to panhandle. For twenty years of homelessness, I had shaken my head at people who stood on corners. In my distorted worldview, stealing was better. Prostitution was better. Anything was better, *anything*, than standing on the street, in full view of everyone, and begging for a dime.

So that's where God sent me: to the street corner for one hour, every day, rain or shine. He sent me not for the money. He sent me not to be discovered by *Today*—that happened months later by accident—but to humble me. And believe me, I was humbled. I was humbled when people rolled down their window to yell "Get a job, n*gger," or threw soda cans at my head, or when my own grown children drove by and looked the other way so they wouldn't have to acknowledge their daddy, the bum.

So, yes, I cringe when I see that YouTube video, because I see a man as low as any man can ever go. But I smile, too, because I see a man who's trying. I see a man who's turned it over to his Higher Power, who's walking (slowly, slowly) in the way of the

Lord, who's facing his demons in the only way he knows how. I was in pain. I was embarrassed. But that pain and embarrassment was the reawakening of things I thought I'd killed off long before: Self-respect. Hope. And love. Especially love.

More than anything, though, I'm grateful. I'm grateful to Doral Chenoweth, the videographer from *The Columbus Dispatch* who took that video; and I'm grateful to the forty million people (and counting) who viewed it, because that video changed my life. On January 4, 2011, the day I became a YouTube sensation, I didn't know what YouTube was. I didn't know what the Internet was, because I'd been homeless since 1993, long before most people went online. Not only had I never touched a computer, I didn't know MTV had more than one channel. I didn't know hip-hop and Rush Limbaugh had taken over the radio. I'd never even heard of Fox News, Mos Def, or Conan O'Brien. Like many homeless people, I had a pay-as-you-go cell phone, which I periodically bought minutes for, but otherwise, twenty years of technology and culture had passed me by.

Twenty years of life had passed me by.

So when my friend Mark called and told me, "They been talking about you on the radio," I was shocked. "Everybody's looking for you," Mark said. "Everybody wants to hear that golden voice."

"You joking me?"

"Nah, it's true."

Man, I got excited. I used to be the number one morning-drive DJ in Columbus, Ohio, and when I heard *radio* I thought someone wanted to give me a job. Radio was my identity—it was even my name on the street—but I hadn't been on the radio since 1996. A radio job meant a hot meal, clean water, a place to live, a shower, a toothbrush, an indoor toilet, but more than that it meant the end of humiliation, the end of degradation, and the return of a decent life.

So I called my friend Al Battle, the only person I knew with a car.

"They're talking about me on the radio, Al. They're telling me to come to WNCI tomorrow morning. Can you drive me?"

I spent that night on a stranger's couch. Didn't take a shower because I didn't want to impose. When Al picked me up on my begging corner, Interstate 71 and Hudson, I was huddled in the same camouflage coat I'd worn every day that winter.

"There must be someone famous down here," Al said when we pulled into the station parking lot and saw the camera crews and television trucks.

We walked into the studio, and *bam*, I was mobbed. "You okay, Ted? You need anything? You mind if we call you Ted?"

"No, sir."

"Well, you better comb your hair, Ted. You'll be on the *Dave & Jimmy* show in five minutes, and there's a live television feed to the *Today* Show in New York."

"What?"

"You're world famous, man, didn't you know? Everybody wants to hear from the homeless man with the golden voice."

Next thing I knew, I was on the air. I don't know what I said, but people liked it, I guess, because halfway through the show the Cleveland Cavaliers offered me a PR announcer job. Then a voice-over agent from California said he could make me a million dollars. A million dollars! That was too much. The day before, I'd been a panhandler. Half an hour before, I'd been an anonymous homeless guy walking into a local radio station, praying for $200 voice-over work.

Now I was . . . famous? All those television trucks outside were . . . for me?

The live feed to *Today* didn't work. So they came up with a new plan. They were flying me to New York City *right now*, so I could appear in the studio the next morning.

I didn't have an ID. I hadn't had an official identity, apart from a prison record, for more than a decade. *Today* had to take me to the courthouse for registration, then a homeless shelter for proof of residency, then the DMV—where we were allowed to cut to the front of the line . . . at the DMV!—for a driver's license, because that was the only way they'd let me on an airplane.

But the next morning, there I was, from the outhouse to the penthouse, saying those famous words to millions nationwide with my golden voice: "From NBC News, this is *Today* with Matt Lauer and Meredith Viera, live from Studio 1A in Rockefeller Plaza."

Then I sat down beside Matt Lauer (who, I admitted a few days later on *Late Night with Jimmy Fallon,* had "brought out the woman in me") for a ten-minute interview. I had a haircut, a clean shave, and a new green sweater, but I was still wearing my camouflage jacket. I was still Ted Williams, the man from the street.

And the most important thing I told the world, after the confessions and tears, was this: "I was ready to mark 2010 as another year wasted, until I realized that in 2010 I found a new spirituality."

I know some people doubt me. I know some people hate my sudden fame and all it says about the media today. They say I didn't earn it. They say I didn't work, that I am the laborer who arrived at the last minute of the day. They say I'm going to relapse. They said, even then, I wouldn't last a week.

But I've made it so far. I'm taking it one day at a time, and I'm making it so far. I'm getting out of bed in the morning (a bed!) and drinking coffee, like a regular Joe. And my spirituality is the reason. You see, I wasn't plucked from the streets in the depth of my addiction and depression. I wasn't dragged off the corner at rock bottom. I was found at a moment of hope, when my heart was open and my spirit was trying to be free.

That's the story I'm going to tell in this book. Not the fame, but the journey: the bad, the worse, the truly ugly, and eventually the not so bad, the getting better, and finally . . . on the very last page, the good. Not the fame, but the good.

Momma, forgive me for the story I'm about to tell. Patty, forgive me for the heartache and betrayal. Children, forgive me for the awful things my grandchildren will hear and the awful things I've done to you. I've made mistakes. I've squandered your love. I've hurt you all, and I know it will hurt you again to hear this litany of sins.

But I've got a second chance, and I've got to come clean. I've got to be honest about what happened and what I've done. My recovery demands it, and my faith demands it, too.

There are thousands of people like me. There are millions in pain, in need, with a poverty of the mind and soul. I'm not just talking about the homeless, although I care about them most of all. I'm talking about anyone who knows they are doing wrong, from the lying businessman to the cheating spouse. I want to reach out a hand and tell them: There is hope. There is redemption. There is a way.

I want to give back to the people who recognized me and said "Way to go, Ted!" The people who smiled and shook my hand, when a few weeks before I was so dirty people changed lanes in their cars to avoid being near me, and said "God bless you, Ted. God bless you." I want to give an honest account for the people who yell, even today, when I walk down the street, "We're proud of you, Ted. We're *proud* of you. We're rooting for you!"

Most important, I want to help the people who are hurting, who have lost their jobs, or their homes, or their families or children, or even their hope. I want to tell this story, not for myself but for the woman who hugged me in the Columbus airport and cried on my shoulder.

"My daughter's a dopehead, Ted," she said. "My daughter's lost, and I've been praying so long and so hard. Why hasn't God answered my prayers?"

"Don't stop," I told her through my own tears. "Don't stop, Momma. Don't stop. My momma prayed for me since 1989, so don't stop. Don't lose your faith. If God can save me, He can save anybody."

CHAPTER 1

had a happy childhood, or at least as happy as anyone else. If you're looking for an explanation for what happened later, don't look there. My momma loved me from the moment she saw me in the newborn room at St. Mary's Hospital. She taught me manners and morals. Every Sunday, I woke up early with her to attend eight A.M. Sunday school at Berean Baptist Church, followed most weeks by the adult service soon after. Berean Baptist was one of those big old-school cathedrals, like in *The Blues Brothers,* with a dancing choir and light streaming in the stained glass windows and James Brown in the pulpit. I'd watch in amazement as the congregation whooped and hollered, and the minister threw up his hands and exhorted the believers, in an unforgettable voice, to praise the Lord. Momma took me to Berean Baptist every Wednesday for Cub Scout meetings, too, even though me and my friend Lowell were the only two boys from our huge housing development who participated. She placed a firm hand—in support, but also in discipline—on everything I did. She was a black working-class housewife in the late 1950s, already past forty years old, and I was her miracle child. But it was those Sunday-morning spectacles, as much as her steady example, that stayed with me.

Most kids in the great African-American melting pot of Bedford-Stuyvesant, Brooklyn, where we lived in the Kingsborough housing project, never left the neighborhood. My momma was different; she wanted me to experience the world. She took me to Rockefeller Center and the Statue of Liberty. She dressed me in nice shorts and high socks, imitating the Kennedy kids, who were all the rage in white America at the time. She took me to museums. We ate at Jack Dempsey's—and the smiling photo of us in a plush booth doesn't quite capture the fact that I ate steak as she ate the cheapest salad. But it does capture the big smiles of a skinny boy in pressed clothes and a well-dressed, dignified woman.

That was Miss Julia Williams. Dignified. Always dignified. She carried herself with a pride that some of our neighbors, and thus their children, found aloof. I admit she could be a little cold, because that's how dignified people behaved, but she always warmed to me because I made her laugh. I gave her a companion and a purpose, a reason to be proud. It was never spend, spend, spend when we were out on the town because we didn't have much money, but she always treated me like a little man, let me talk and joke and drink soda pop, then hugged me to her and told me "I love you, Teddy," on the subway ride home.

It was different when my dad was with us. He worked hard, often on evening and weekend shifts, so he usually wasn't around for our trips. We went to Rockaway Beach with Daddy once every summer, and Coney Island with him twice a year, where he always insisted I eat Nathan's hot dogs. He was like that: very rule-bound. "When people come to Coney Island," he said, "they eat Nathan's hot dogs, so that's what we're gonna eat."

Well, I hated Nathan's hot dogs. So when my father wasn't look-ing, my mother would slip me a dollar and tell me to run and get my favorite.

"Where'd you get those frog legs, boy?"

"Oh, Al," my momma would say. "Teddy must have saved his money."

Momma didn't stand up to my father much. Whether it was his drinking or his discipline, it was usually just "Now, Al, that's enough," like it was only too much butter on the beans. Our neigh-bor Miss Brown was usually the one who stepped between my daddy and me, but Momma was the one who was there for me to fall asleep against, full and happy, when the clanging subway car carried us back from Coney Island to Bed-Stuy.

There were kids in the neighborhood who didn't like that, especially after we started traveling. My father was a baggage handler at Eastern Airlines, so we could fly first class to California for eleven dollars round trip. We went to Hawaii, Puerto Rico, Miami Beach. The other kids never rode the subway, much less went to Bermuda (Momma's favorite, because everyone dressed up for dinner), and they resented my momma's attention. And my nice clothes. And my light skin.

"Your momma's stuck up," they'd say. "She thinks she's whiter than the rest of us."

Maybe Momma was haughty. I'm not saying she wasn't, because she knew how to look down her nose. She believed in the better-ment of the race, but Booker T.–style, not Malcolm X. Most of her friends were "high-yellow" homemakers like herself. I know that's a slavery term for light-skinned blacks, but it was still in vogue in the "Black Is Beautiful" days of the 1960s, when the tone of your black skin defined you, and the darker the better. Even during the civil rights movement, when police were beating black men right on our street, Momma wore blonde wigs under her Jackie Kennedy hats and dressed up every day because she cared how she looked. Those kids in the hood thought she was high society, because they'd never seen real high society, and that's how Momma carried herself. They didn't know Julia Williams came from a sharecropping farm in rural Ohio, that her momma died when she was six months old, and that her father made her drop out of school in seventh grade. "You know how to read and write, that's all you need to be a housekeeper," her father told her. He didn't mean a paid housekeeper. He meant a maid for himself and his new wife.

Her aunt in Columbus, Ohio, rescued her. Took her out of that house and put her back in school. "You're not too smart, Julia," her aunt told my momma, "but you're clean and you're honest, and that will take you far."

My mother took those words to heart. Cleanliness. Honesty. That was her calling in life. She was light skinned, and she learned right then she could elevate herself beyond her humble upbringing with dignity alone. She learned to walk with her head up, to iron her clothes, and to keep her white gloves clean. Just out of high school she got a job as an elevator operator at Lazarus, the nicest department store in Columbus. That was the tip-top for a black girl in those days; they hired only the classiest high-yellow Negroes for that job. I'm tempted to say the most Uncle Tom, since those girls were chosen to appeal to white customers, but I know that's a bitterness in me. My momma raised herself from shackles by straightening her spine, and who am I to question that strength?

She met my father on a visit to Harlem. She was at an aunt's house, sitting on a pillow in the window looking at the people out strolling, when she said, "I know that man, Auntie. He's from Columbus."

The next time he walked by, because that's what black folks did in Harlem in the 1930s, they strolled up and down the avenues, she went down and introduced herself. Within a few weeks Al Williams was taking her to the Savoy and the Apollo. They got married and moved into a five-dollar-a-week hall room, which was nothing but a bed, a chest, and a shared bathroom at the end of the hall. My father followed the Yankees and my momma followed the fashions, because she loved the way those Harlem women dressed. She never forgot those women, even after they moved to Bedford-Stuyvesant in the 1940s to be closer to my father's job in a paint factory, because for her that was the life black people could aspire to. She settled into a two-bedroom apartment in the new city-owned housing development, with its identical towers set among green lawns and fresh young trees. She decked the place out in inexpensive, stylish furniture, found some like-minded friends, and waited fifteen years for the baby to come. But the baby never came.

By the late 1950s, she was that woman. You know the one. The polite older lady who looks after the neighborhood kids. The quiet conscience of the floor, nice but not afraid to speak her mind. The person everyone secretly thinks, before they take that shortcut in life, "I shouldn't do that, now—Ms. Williams won't approve." And then they resent her for it. She was the woman every child in the second building of the fourth walk of the Kingsborough Houses called by her first name, Ms. Julia; and many thought of as their second mother, especially the Brown kids, who lived next door.

"I'd give you my kids if I could," Mrs. Brown, her best friend, sometimes told my mother. "They're at your apartment more than mine anyway."

And then one day, instead of making a joke, she said, "I can't give you my kids, Julia, but I know a woman who's getting ready to have a baby, and she don't want it."

That was the neighborhood. The white world wasn't going to help, so you had to take care of your own. If there was a young single mother with three kids already and a baby she'd been drinking water and eating apples to try to kill off inside her, and a woman who wanted kids more than anything but never could have them, well, there was every reason to put them together.

"Don't get your hopes up, Julia," Al Williams told her. "Ain't nobody gonna give you a baby just because you don't have one."

A few weeks later, when someone hollered up to her window, "It's a boy, Ms. Julia. He's at the hospital, and if you don't come get him, the momma's going to leave him there." My momma hesitated only at the word *boy*. She'd always wanted a girl. But she showed up an hour later with new baby clothes, and that's how I became Ted Fred Williams, the one and only child of Julia and Al Williams of Brooklyn, New York.

I can't fault my momma for anything, really, except never telling me where I came from. She didn't hide that I was adopted, but whenever I asked her about my birth mother, she'd say, "You got a momma who loves you now, what you want to know about that woman for?"

I never even knew my birth mother's name. I never met her, even though she lived only a few blocks away. I heard my momma say once, "She couldn't be bothered," and I've never forgotten those words. My real mother *couldn't be bothered* to raise her own child. She couldn't be bothered to visit, not once. She just handed me to Julia Williams, said "God bless you," and disappeared from my life. When she saw us coming down the street, our neighbor Mrs. Brown told me later, my real mother turned the other way before my new momma noticed her. Everybody in the neighborhood saw it but Momma, because she was too busy looking at me.

When I found out my birth mother had other kids she was raising, I was crushed. "Not one of them has ever come looking for me, Momma," I said, crying.

"Oh, child," Momma said, giving me a big hug. "Maybe they're too young. Maybe they don't know about you. God gave you to me, Teddy. You should be happy with what we have."

But I couldn't be happy, not with that hole in my heart, even though God had given me the best momma in Bed-Stuy. I kept asking about my real mother, the other woman, the one who had given me away. I asked until it hurt me to ask anymore, until my adoptive momma felt sorry for me. I could see it in her eyes when she held me, when she shook her head and said, "I don't know, Teddy. I don't know why she didn't want you."

It didn't help that I was strange-looking, that in an all-black neighborhood—I knew of only four white families in the Kingsborough Houses—I didn't quite look like everyone else. The other kids would say, "We don't know what you is. One day you're playing with us, the next day it's the Port-o Ricans—we don't know what you is."

"Now, Teddy," my momma said, "they don't even know how to talk, so don't pay no attention to them."

I heard it all the time from everyone. One time a grown woman came up to me on the street, I must have been five or six, and asked, "What are you, boy?"

I turned to her and said, dead serious, "I am a full American."

My momma laughed about that for years; told that story a hundred times. But I wasn't laughing. And Momma shouldn't have been either. After all, the first caseworker that came to our apartment said, "You can't adopt this baby, Ms. Williams. You're black, and this baby's white." Momma had to go to a special doctor in Manhattan to have me declared mixed race, because that's how serious color was in those days. My whole life turned on the question of race—and hers did, too.

My father, though, knew all along what I was, or what I should claim to be. "Don't have nothing to do with the black man, son," Al Williams told me. "The black man is low. He has nothing to offer. Don't ever tell nobody your race. Just let them assume. If anybody asks, you tell them white."

I can't blame him for that. Not really. Al Williams came from the most color-struck family I've ever known. My mother's family was a rainbow, all mixed, but on my father's side, they had separate reunions for the light-skinned and the dark. I had uncles and cousins who went to their grave thinking they were less than, just because of the color of their skin. My father was a dark-skinned black man, about ten shades darker than his almost identical brother, and he hated that biological mistake all his life. He processed his hair like Cab Calloway so he could comb it straight with an Ace comb—always an Ace comb. He tried to pass for Samoan or Hawaiian, anything but the rural American Negro he was.

He worked like a dog, too, to make up for his birth. I don't think he missed a day of work, not in thirty years at Eastern Airlines, and I doubt he ever arrived late. He never missed a chance to show his bosses he was twice as responsible and twice as tireless as any white man tossing luggage into their shiny new planes. But he never got anywhere. He got plaques to put on the wall—so many months of perfect attendance, so many years of honorable service— and free travel vouchers, but he never got promoted. He was always just a bag man. No matter how "yessir" my daddy was to his bosses, he knew in his heart, at the end of the day, they were calling him "n*gger" behind his back, and that ate the man up inside.

He didn't want that for me. He wanted me to have equal opportunities—by *saying* I was white—and that wasn't popular in Bed-Stuy in the 1960s. Black Is Beautiful, that was the rallying cry. And the blacker the better. On the day Martin Luther King Jr. was shot, a boy at school turned to me and said, "You better run home, Ted. You better not look back, because the man who killed Martin Luther King don't look like me. He looks like you." My parents laughed when I told them, but I was terrified. In elementary school, they asked us to draw a picture of what we wanted to be when we grew up. I drew a black man. Not a black fireman. Not a black policeman. Just a black man. With an earring.

Not that I wasn't popular. I got picked on for my skin color, and my giant glasses, and also my mouth, which never stopped flapping, but I was always surrounded by other kids. It was an obsession for me, to be around friends. I've always been a giver, a guy who gathers people together. Even when I was on my knees in the crack house, I was a giver, and a crack house is the most selfish place on earth. When I was a kid, I threw my toys out my window to the neighbor boys, because I knew they didn't have any. I bought everyone candy, because I was the only one with change in my pocket. I befriended Otis, the kid who smelled bad and always wore the same clothes because his momma sat all day in a bar. Otis would have dinner at our apartment a couple times a week. I took a boy in the building on the subway one day, because he'd never been out of the neighborhood. I was nine; he was five. We didn't get back until after dark. My daddy put welts on my hide for that one, but that boy wanted to see the world.

My parents tried. My momma took me to Berean Baptist, my

father wore my rear end out. But it never helped. I was a pleaser. I kept hanging out on the corner with the wrong kids, at least according to my parents. I kept lingering down the block after my father whistled me home. I was supposed to be home every day at five o'clock sharp for dinner. The other kids knew that, and when they heard my daddy's whistle they'd beg me to go home, just go home, because they knew the consequences. But I didn't care; I'd come home late. My daddy would whip me, and Momma would say, "I can't help it, Teddy. Those are Daddy's rules. You know how he is."

My momma wanted to send me to private school. She thought it might straighten me out. My father objected. "I didn't go to private school, you didn't go to private school, and we turned out fine."

"The world's different now, Al."

She was a teacher's aide in the public school, so she saw it every day: the fights over skin color and glasses, kids getting beat up because their momma bought them a new jacket from a store, not a hand-me-down.

Daddy wouldn't pay for it—Al Williams put $150 on the table for my momma every Friday, and that was all he was willing to give—so my momma took a higher-paying job as a school cafeteria worker to pay for my private education. Can you imagine Julia Williams, the classiest high-yellow woman on the block, slopping food in a cafeteria line in her perfectly pressed uniform, just to send her wayward boy to religious school?

And it never even crossed my mind to thank her.

Even in religious school, away from so-called bad influences, I was the class clown. The teachers would send notes home: *Good work when we can get it, but he won't sit still. He talks all the time. I can't get him to focus.* My father wore me out over those notes, but I couldn't help it. If I met you, I had to talk to you. Shake your hand.

Make you laugh. Give you a hug if you were feeling down. I loved Narcotics Anonymous meetings for that reason, because there was so much hugging. In rehab, they said my outgoing nature was a defense mechanism, that I was hiding my feelings behind my personality, and I'm sure that's true. But that doesn't mean it's not me. For better or worse, I was the kid who yelled funny comments in class and made up goofy lyrics to popular songs. I was the kid on the corner trying the latest dance move while the other kids clapped along.

Then, when I was ten, my father became a Jehovah's Witness. It was a strain on my parents' marriage, because Momma would never give up Berean Baptist, but for me it was an opportunity. My father was a sports nut, especially baseball. That's why he named me after Ted Williams, a man who the year I was born played for the last all-white team in major league baseball. My father dreamed of having a baseball player for a son, but I had no aptitude for sports, and we lost that link early on.

There was no reason, though, why I couldn't be a Witness. So I ditched Berean Baptist and tagged along to service with my father. Afterward we'd distribute *The Watchtower*, the Jehovah's Witness publication, in the neighborhood. Several nights a week, my father quizzed me on scripture, and I studied the Bible religiously to make sure I was ready. It wasn't long before I was speaking in front of the congregation, giving five-minute talks on assigned themes, a common practice in that church. I was twelve years old, but my voice was already deep, and I could deliver it as smooth as water. The Jehovah's Witness–style was slow and calm, the exact opposite of Berean Baptist, and nobody delivered the message better than me. My daddy and I were so well known in that church, everybody called me "Little Al." Daddy started taking me along when he umpired high school baseball games, and everyone there called me Little Al, too.

Then, at thirteen, I was caught smoking a cigarette. The trouble wasn't so much the smoking, it was the fact that I was leaning against the Jehovah's Witness temple building when I did it. But, man, was it trouble. If I had been baptized in their faith, which I wasn't, the Witnesses would have kicked me out. As it was, they put me on probation and wouldn't allow me to speak in church. They even cancelled the talk I was to give that very afternoon, on the theme "Are you maintaining your vow to God?"

My father was livid. He said I discredited him with his friends. He said I was an embarrassment to the family. He said all kinds of things I'll never forget, and when we got home that day he said the one thing he said to me more often than any other during my childhood: "Put your glasses aside, boy. Put your glasses aside."

That meant he was about to whip me, and whip me good. I still don't know what he thought would happen if he whipped me with my glasses on, but I remember that day, because I never again walked by my father's side. I don't remember the whipping, but even now, forty years later, I remember every word of the five-minute talk on loyalty to God I'd been planning to give.

CHAPTER 2

When I was ten years old, my momma gave me a little Panasonic radio. She said it was because I was laid up sick in bed, but I suppose it was also her way of keeping me close because that's about the time I drifted away to try and impress my father. Even now she keeps that radio in my old bedroom, like she's waiting for that little boy to return. She doesn't have much from my childhood—a few scrapbooks, three drawings from elementary school—but she has my Panasonic, because that radio *was* my childhood. I listened to it every day.

My father loved sports, but not me. I loved entertainers. When I was in elementary school, my heroes were Soupy Sales, Red Skelton, and Jackie Gleason. I learned voice inflection, the up-and-down sentences, the dramatic pauses and rushes, from endlessly listening to them tell jokes. I learned to imitate people from Rich Little, and for a few years imitations were the centerpiece of my class clowning. I did celebrities, neighborhood busybodies, teachers. Even imitations of my parents, so professional but so dysfunctional, made my whole class laugh. It wasn't nice, I suppose, but it was my talent. For a while, I thought I wanted to be a comedian.

Then I heard the disc jockeys on my little Panasonic radio. Cross-over jocks were big in the late 1960s—white guys like Casey Kasem, who sounded black, and Murray the K, who always played the Temptations. I never pretended to be a baseball player, like my father would have liked, but I used to wear a cape and say "ah big whoop, big whoop" because that was one of Murray the K's catch-phrases. And Murray the K, like everyone on radio in those days, had personality. The voices were big and booming, and they grabbed that space between the songs. Murray the K wasn't just a white man spinning black tunes, he was larger than life, bigger to me than even The Temptations. When I heard him jumping out of windows and crashing to the ground in a jangle of sound effects, it was pure magic. I could see it. I could be it. And it was nothing but the radio.

It was the big black voices on the R&B stations, though, men like Vaughn Harper, that hooked me. I'd listen for hours just to hear Frankie Crocker, the most famous black disc jockey in New York at the time, because he was big, black, proud, and smooth. Just hearing Frankie Crocker say *Mostly cloudy today with afternoon showers* put more ambition in my head than any whipping ever could.

But my favorite disc jockey was Hank Spann. Ask anybody who grew up black in New York City in the 1960s, and they'll remember Hank Spann. He was the morning jock on WWRL, the only AM station for R&B and soul (and nobody in Bedford-Stuyvesant got anything but AM back then). I'd wake up every morning, just like every other black boy in New York (or so I imagined), to the sound of "W-W-R-L, Hank Spann with you, baby, it's gonna be a hot one today."

That's where I got my voice, from Hank Spann. I mean, God gave it to me, but Hank Spann showed me how to use it. There isn't a professional baseball player alive who spent more time working on their gift as a kid than I spent working on mine. When I wasn't studying the Bible to impress my father, I'd sit for hours imitating Hank Spann, dropping that "W-W-R-L" tag over and over again, until my voice sounded just right. And I do mean just right, because the more I imitated Hank Spann, the more my voice deepened and thickened, taking on Hank Spann's honey sound. It was puberty, of course, but it felt like fate.

When I was twelve, just before I fell out of favor with my father, my momma gave me a little plug-in microphone and a tape recorder. It was the best Christmas gift I ever received. I walked around the apartment all day with that microphone, using my radio voice to describe what I saw.

Good afternoon, ladies and gentlemen, this is Ted Williams on W-W-R-L, nothing but the best of soul, and it's gonna be a hot one in the Kingsborough Houses, baby, especially with Momma cooking green beans in the kitchen.

I'd make up my own sign-offs—*Ted Williams here, urging you to keep the faith and rock the soul*—and stand at the window telling my imaginary listeners what was happening outside.

I'd write news copy, then record it twenty times until I got it just right. My father'd be lounging on the sofa, drinking beer, and he'd say, "Take that thing away, Ted, don't nobody want to hear that."

But my mother would say, "Show me what you did, Teddy."

I'd hit the play button, and there was my booming radio voice, saying, "Today in Brooklyn, Ben Berger was badly beaten in the back of Barry's bowling alley. Now here's Bernard Bellman with more."

"It was a terrible tragedy of trauma here on Taylor Street, Ted, when ten troubled teens tangled. . . ."

I never went back to Berean Baptist, even after I left my father's church. I attended services, but I never really went back. I'm not saying that cigarette at the Jehovah temple changed the course of my life. I was always a boy who did his own thing—and why was I smoking at thirteen if I wasn't drifting away? I'm just saying that's the moment I stopped being my momma's boy, or my daddy's boy, and started trying to find my own way. And the thing that guided me then, just as it guides me now, was my voice. My voice was my identity. It was the only thing black about me, for one thing, and I loved it for that reason alone.

It also made me popular. I may have been skinny and four-eyed, I may have been almost white, but women loved the way I talked. Every day at lunch, it was me and eight girls, and I kept them entertained. I was a good dancer, too—in Bed-Stuy, you had to be a lover, a dancer, or an athlete to be somebody, and I was two out of three—but I was an even better emcee. I wasn't dropping rap beats, since this was 1973, but I was running the show. My friends and I would be down on the corner with our radio, clapping and dancing, gathering a crowd, and I'd step to the middle and say, "Ted Williams here, babies, and I'd like you to put your hands together and welcome, right here on Ralph Avenue, for your entertainment, the master himself, the hardest working man in show business . . . the Godfather of Ssss-oul!!" And this boy would jump in and start dancing like James Brown. He even looked like James Brown. Between my emceeing and his dancing, we'd have the whole block happy.

"I'm gonna be on the radio," I told my parents. "A million people gonna hear the sound of my voice."

That was my prayer, for a million people to hear my voice. Not baseball, not business, not even a band. I wanted to be Hank Spann, the disc jockey, because every morning (I imagined) a million people woke up to the sound of his voice.

"That's not a job," my father snorted. "That's just putting a needle on a record."

"Oh, Al," Momma said, shaking her head. "You don't have to be like that."

It didn't matter to me. What did Al Williams know? He loaded luggage.

Hank Spann was a man. He was articulate, but he was macho, you know, big and bad, like a Transformer or something. You could hear it in his voice, the man's balls hung to the floor. God help me, I know it's crude, but I was fourteen years old and that's what I wanted: black balls to the floor.

Then I met him, on a class field trip to WWRL. I remember seeing a man walk out of the booth and thinking, *That ain't Hank Spann. That man's . . . small. Like my father.*

Then he started talking. He had that voice—The Soul Server they called him, The Golden Voice—and I'll never forget the resonance and timbre of it, like chocolate honey. But it was the words Hank Spann said that day that changed my life.

He said: "Radio is defined as theater of mind."

On the radio, he told us, you can create anything you want. And you don't have to make it with wood and glue. You make it with your voice, and it's in the air, baby, because you put it straight into the listener's mind. Look at Amos and Andy, who people thought were black. Look at "War of the Worlds." Orson Welles had people jumping out windows *in real life*, just because of his voice.

And there was something else Hank Spann was saying to me, not with his words but with his small build and light skin—*On the radio, son, you can be anybody you want to be. It doesn't matter what you look like. It doesn't matter if you're skinny, four-eyed, and practically white. All that matters is the sound.*

CHAPTER 3

You'd think I would've looked for work at a radio station. Or applied to broadcasting school. Or got a job somewhere where my voice would be heard. But it just wasn't done in my neighborhood, thinking ahead and pursuing a career like that, and I didn't have parents to lead me. By the time I was in high school, there was too much space between us. They sat in the apartment listening to Count Basie and sipping drinks with their well-dressed friends, like they were back in Harlem, 1935. I was on the street corner dancing and emceeing with my friends, pure Bed-Stuy, 1973.

My father valued work, and not much else. He was a workaholic. "Show me a dollar" was the first thing he said every time he saw me. "Show me a dollar, son." And he didn't mean a pocketful of change; he meant a dollar bill. If my friends and I couldn't reach in our pockets and each pull out a dollar bill, he'd shake his head. A man ain't nothing without a dollar in this pocket, that's what Al Williams believed.

I didn't mind working for my dollars. In fact, I loved it. By ten, I was a newspaper boy. I collected bottles and shined shoes. In the middle of a streetball game, I'd drop what I was doing and run an errand for someone in the building (they yelled out their windows for me), because they let me keep the change. I was buying cigarettes at eleven years old, no problem, because the clerks knew I was the pickup boy for the Kingsborough Houses. If there was a job to be done for spare change, from pumping gas to picking up that order Mrs. Thompson or Mrs. Ginn called in to the butcher, Teddy was the man. Every Saturday I went to the grocery store with Mrs. Brown, because that was my big payday, two dollars per trip. And I didn't stop there. I took that money and bought flip books and candy bars, which I sold for twice the price at school. I mastered trading baseball cards, strictly for the cash, and many days those cardboard cards put the dollar bills in my pockets that my father was so eager to see.

But Al Williams wasn't impressed, either with my radio ambitions or my entrepreneurship. To him, a man worked a steady job for a steady paycheck and came home every night to his dinner and his beer. A man didn't dream of the radio, and he certainly didn't hustle on the streets. My father earned his dollars the old-fashioned way, day in and day out, but that seemed like sucker work to me. That effort, to me, made him bitter. He told me no black man would ever get ahead in a white man's world, and then he proved it every day.

So I defied my father and, at seventeen, took the fastest way out of the neighborhood for a black boy in 1975: I joined the United States Army. That was the first time I broke my momma's heart. She cried, I remember that clearly, because I'd never seen her cry before. She wanted me to finish high school. But my parents were moving to a new neighborhood because the stairways in the Kingsborough Houses smelled like piss, which was my momma's way of saying Bedford-Stuyvesant wasn't what it used to be, and I didn't want to follow them. What was I going to do in Crown Heights? And besides, I was friends with the recruiter, Sergeant Vega. I worked with him for a year, processing paperwork, handing out flyers, talking about my dreams, and he finally sold me on a career as a communications specialist. He had it mapped out: five years for Ted Williams from enlistment to a 71 Romeo MOS—a radio and television broadcast man for the Armed Forces Korea Network.

I barely made it through basic training. It wasn't the clowning that brought me down, because I knew the army didn't tolerate that. It was the hustle. By the time our first paychecks hit three weeks into training, I was starving, primarily because I kept failing the horizontal bars portion of physical training, and they wouldn't let me eat until I passed. So I got four brothers together, and I talked them into pooling our paychecks. My team happened to be on patrol that night, so I took the money, snuck out to the PX and bought Ho Hos, potato chips, gummy bears, chocolate milk. I figured I could turn four hundred dollars into a thousand by morning, but instead of a room full of eager recruits, I walked into a dead bunkhouse. Not a sound. Not a light. Then somebody coughed, and I noticed Drill Sergeant Buzzard—and yes, that was his real name—standing in the dark.

"What'd you bring me, meat?"

Oh, man, now that was a voice. It brought the whole world down around me. You could have heard a mouse fart.

"Food, sir."

He took me to his office, pulled out the stuff he wanted, and set it aside. "Now eat it, recruit."

"Eat what, sir?"

"The rest of it, meat."

I ate for an hour. Oreos. Goobers. Chocolate chip cookies. At

the end, he was literally pouring chocolate milk down my throat.
He stuffed me like a turkey until I was about to burst, then sent me
to my bunk. But I kept my wits. I knew Buzzard would kick me out
in the morning, so before I went to bed—and I didn't sleep a minute, not after ten pounds of Twinkies—I set a picture of my beautiful, light-skinned cousin on top of my foot locker.

Sure enough, Buzzard came storming in at 0500, ready to chew
my face off. "At attention, meat." He called us that all the time:
meat. Nothing but meat. I hoisted myself up and came this close to
puking on his dog tags. He looked at me in disgust. Then he noticed my cousin's picture.

"Who is that, recruit?"

"That is my sister, sir."

"Is she coming to your graduation?"

"If I make it, sir."

He paused. "All right, meat," he said. "Give me two hundred."

It wasn't easy, not with those Twinkies . . . and Ho Hos . . . and
Oreos sloshing in my stomach, but I made it, and even my father
was proud when he saw my clipped hair and dress whites at graduation. He was already talking about the pension I could get when I
retired, and how I should invest it.

"Are these your parents, Private Williams?"

"Yes, sir, Drill Sergeant Buzzard."

"And where is your sister, recruit?"

"Oh, Teddy doesn't have a sister," my momma said helpfully.
"He's an only child."

Drill Sergeant Buzzard took it like a man. He looked at me like
I was real meat this time, the dead kind, but he said simply, "Private Williams, before you go, please show your parents front leaning position."

I got down for a push-up.

"Now low crawl, recruit. Low crawl."

And I did. I crawled across the parade ground on my belly in my dress whites in front of my entire company. My father thought it was hilarious. "First time I've seen you take orders, boy," he said with a laugh. That was the first day since I quit the Witnesses—the very first—I ever thought he was proud of me.

Even Drill Sergeant Buzzard smiled in the end. "You're going to be all right, private," he told me, shaking my hand. "You're going to be all right."

But I wasn't. Sergeant Vega neglected to tell me when I enlisted that there was a typing test to be a communication specialist, and I didn't know how to type. So I flunked the test, and instead of communications, the army assigned me to truck maintenance for the 650th, an environmental sanitation unit that drove around Korea checking the relative cleanliness of mess halls, barber shops, and latrines. In other words, I was a mechanic for the South Korea outhouse patrol.

I'd like to say the assignment sunk me, and in a way it did. My father would have embraced that challenge, worked hard every day . . . and maybe advanced two ranks in ten years. Not me. I saw a decade of meaningless work, with no radio at the end, and I fell into depression, and then into drink. That's what sunk me. My attitude, and especially my drinking.

Ever since I started sipping the dregs before refilling my father's cocktails when I was eight years old, I've had a drinking problem. I don't know what it was about alcohol, but I took to it immediately. I've said it before, and I'll say it again: Crack saved my life. I never took pills or acid, never sniffed anything up my nose or shot anything into my veins. It was alcohol for me, then crack; and if crack hadn't come along, I'd be a drooling idiot with wet brain by now. That's how much I loved the taste of liquor. No, not the taste, but the way it made me feel: like I could dance when I was thirteen, and the older boys handed me beers for special routines. Or like I was fitting in, when I tried cheap wine with my friends at fifteen. Or like I was finally independent, at sixteen, when I bought half a pint of vodka every morning with my lunch money—I'd sit with the girls at lunch and pick food off their plates, because high school girls never ate what the school served them—and finished the bottle before the end of the day. By then, I realize now, drinking was my way of escaping childhood, and God help me, it wasn't just my daddy's belt I was running from, it was also that sheltered little kid who fell asleep happy on his momma's lap with his belly full of frog legs.

In Korea, stuck in the Seoul depot while most of my unit poked around latrines, I drank, and I drank heavy. It was a big base right in the middle of the city, and there were always new soldiers with money to burn. I was the perfect guide and companion, a talker, a raconteur, and a comedian with as many imitations in the army as I had in Catholic school. And even better for most of those eighteen-year-old recruits, I was familiar with the darker parts of Seoul.

Pretty soon, I started serving more than their guide needs. If they needed anything—a radio, a pocketknife, a magazine or album to remind them of home—I supplied it. I bought the items in town and, usually, traded them to the soldiers for their monthly allotments. Each soldier, for instance, was given eight ounces of black pepper each month, but most soldiers didn't want it. So I traded two-dollar magazines for their pepper and sold it in the city, 50 ounces for $350. For black pepper! By the end of the year, I was carrying a case of gonorrhea, two Article 15s—pay reduction and loss of rank—and a strong suspicion from my commanding officer that I was a black-marketeer. I wouldn't call it that, since I was only giving my fellow soldiers what they wanted, but my conduct was certainly unbecoming, even for a private. By the time my eighteen-month evaluation rolled around, I was in trouble over some Bose stereo equipment I had sold without authorization. If I couldn't produce that stereo, I was staring at a possible court-martial.

Fortunately, I was popular with the officers, despite my proclivities, because I was always joking and dropping my radio voice on them, which was my real voice, only two octaves deeper and twice as smooth. I was buttering them up, sure, but I genuinely liked them, too. I had a fantasy that one of them was going to stop and say, "Boy, with that voice, you shouldn't be changing tires, you should be on armed forces radio." That didn't happen, of course, but my CO liked me enough to decide the better course of action, both for the army and myself, was to simply part ways. So I took the dishonorable discharge and headed back to the United States with nothing in my pockets but some penicillin and a bag of black pepper.

I headed first to Brooklyn, but my father was still hung up on that army pension, and my momma was too disappointed to welcome me home. So I took the bus to North Carolina, where my best friend from high school had moved. Lowell was still in the army—we'd enlisted together—so I lived with his brother in Whiteville, a small town just north of Myrtle Beach, South Carolina, whose name was also an accurate description. I worked for a while on a Department of Transportation road crew. Shoveling asphalt and roadkill wasn't a bad job, but it wasn't the life for me, so I kept my ear to the ground. When I heard about a job opening at WVOE radio in nearby Chadbourn, I applied.

No, I didn't just apply. I went over and just about beat the door down.

WVOE was a small country place, no bigger than a double-wide trailer. It didn't even have a paved parking lot, but that wasn't surprising because this was a small Negro town in the Deep South (it was on the highway outside Chadbourn, twenty years later, that Michael Jordan's father was killed), and hardly any of the local roads were paved. WVOE was just a studio and a reception area, nothing to write home about, as they say, but it was real civilian radio, with gold records on the walls, and I was working for pay. In other words, it was my heaven. Walking into the control room, I felt like God had set me on the path. I'd prayed for a million ears to hear my voice, and He had answered my prayers. There weren't a million ears in Chadbourn, North Carolina, not even close, but I was on my way.

The main disc jockey, Doc Holliday, took me under his wing and showed me how to be a professional radio man: cue the tracks, cut the commercials, make my voice big and bold, like I was preaching to a choir. I worked Sunday afternoon, doing the Top 40 R&B countdown, and it wasn't long before I was talking with station management about a daily shift. I'd been down, but suddenly all that practice, all those years of training my voice on my tape recorder, had paid off. I drank in the juke joints on Saturdays, but I was in church Sunday mornings, and on the air Sunday afternoons, and nothing could stop me. That's how I felt, nothing at all.

Then I got a call in the booth: "Hey, Brother T," a woman's voice said, because that was my radio name. "You look good in that blue suit."

"Thank you, sister, but how do you know what I'm wearing?"

"I live across the street from you. I watch you walking to work. Why don't you let me come pick you up, since you don't have a car?"

"All right," I told her. "Meet me in the lobby at four o'clock."

I don't know what I was expecting, but I wasn't expecting Mary. I mean, the girl was a knockout. Dark and luscious, nice smile, body like a . . . well, needless to say, I got into her car. Instead of turning toward our street, though, she took a turn out into the country and went down a dirt road. She parked the car, put a blanket on the ground, and took off all her clothes. I was nineteen. I'd been with girls in high school, and I'd been with prostitutes in Korea, but I'd never seen a beautiful girl drop her clothes in full daylight before.

Ladies and gentlemen, it was temptation in its most ancient form. And I seized it, not only in body, but in soul. And you don't have to be a genius, or a Christian, or a person of upright moral standing, to realize that wasn't going to end well. That wasn't the kind of relationship that ends years later in the living room of a nice house, with your little son looking up from a puzzle and asking, "So, Daddy, how did you meet Momma anyway?"

So how bad did it get? Well, I fell in love with that girl—or at least I thought I did. I took her into my life and started hitting the bootleg houses, where the liquor was fifty cents a glass. The boys in there didn't like my hands on Mary since I was light-skinned and she was dark, and they were even darker. If it was the old days, they'd have been field hands and I'd have been the house n*gger (if I hadn't been lynched for my big mouth, that is), and there's a natural resentment there, especially when it came to women. Many a night my voice alone saved me from a beating, and after I was promoted to five days a week at WVOE, it was my voice that earned my discount liquor and acceptance, maybe even respect. And that's when I started living. That's when I started feeling strong. God? I forgot about Him. What did I need God for? I wasn't skinny old Ted Williams, I was Brother T, and I had balls to the floor.

Then Mary wrote some bad checks and got in trouble with a loan shark. I was naïve. I didn't know anything was wrong until she skipped town to Baltimore and started writing letters, begging me to join her. I resisted for a few months, since I had my dream job, but eventually I started to picture it: me, Mary, a little house and a dog, and a radio gig in a bigger market somewhere. It was pride, really, because I thought I was special. It was pride and lust.

So I quit WVOE, bought a one-way bus ticket to Baltimore, and of course the relationship fell apart in about ten minutes. Before I knew what hit me, I was back at my parents' house in Brooklyn with no money and no job. When I asked my parents for bus fare back to North Carolina, my father put his foot down.

"No way. Not for some d*mn radio job."

I got angry. I saw the life I wanted, and I saw my father standing in my way. So I stole his credit card and ran up four thousand dollars in charges before the law caught up to me in a motel in eastern North Carolina. Defrauding the innkeeper was the official charge. They locked me up in the Elizabethtown jail for a few weeks, then sent me to the penitentiary in Wilmington. I was sentenced to the reintegration program, a special unit for first-time nonviolent offenders, housed in a separate trailer complex on the far side of the prison yard, but there was a paperwork snafu and I had to do sixty days in the general population.

My cellmate was a black dude who had killed two teenagers at a Friendly's restaurant and stuffed their bodies in the freezer. I was terrified. Not a little bit, but down to my soul. This dude was big, and five minutes after lights out, he started howling. I guess he was torn in two with guilt, or maybe visions of hell, because he howled in torment, he thrashed in the bed, and he screamed all night. I couldn't sleep. Everybody comes into prison with rape-terror, I think, especially a young light-skinned boy like me, but I had murder-terror, too. I was sure as soon as I closed my eyes, that demon was going to snap and beat me to death with his bare hands.

By the second month I couldn't take it anymore. I was insane from fear and lack of sleep, so I slid under the reintegration trailer during yard and waited until the guards were hustling everyone back to their cells. Then I climbed a chain wire fence, threw a blanket over the first loop of double barbed-wire, and scrambled through the foot-wide opening to the other side. I cut my arms and my pants were practically torn off, but I was in the woods before head count was over, and I don't think they noticed I was gone until lights out. I made it all the way to Whiteville before they caught me. This time, they threw me in Warrenton, the maximum security prison. My original sentence was three months, but I ended up spending most of 1979 locked up.

I only found out later—and by later, I mean while writing this book—that the sheriff in Elizabethtown, where I was arrested, had taken a liking to me. He even called my parents and asked them to drop the charges. "He's a good boy," the sheriff told them. "He's young. He just made a mistake." He called every day for a week, in fact, hoping to change their minds. By the time I was scheduled for Wilmington, he was pleading. "You don't want to do that to your boy. He's not cut out for prison. It could ruin his life."

"No, sir," my momma told him, because Momma always answered the call. I can see her now, standing in her kitchen with her arms crossed and her lips pursed. "He's got to take responsibility, sheriff. I'm sorry, I love him, but he's got to pay for what he's done."

CHAPTER 4

I t's easy to be prayerful in prison. You thank God every night for another day without violence. You pray to Jesus to protect you against tomorrow. There are no atheists in the foxhole, people say, but there are haters in the joint. Everybody calls on God in the lion's den, except the lions, and I've never been that kind of hard case. Now that I've been to jail fifteen or sixteen times, I'm used to it. I don't sweat like I did then. I recognize the lions, and I know the difference between the guys praying for a favor and the guys serious about turning their lives around. I thought back then I was the second kind. And in many ways I was, because I was ashamed. I stole from the man who raised me. I lied to the woman who loved me. I stopped praying, stopped being humble, and quit on myself. I turned away from God and my momma's teachings. And I felt bad.

But neither God nor Momma turned away from me. My father wouldn't talk to me while I was locked up, but Momma came all the way to North Carolina to tell me she loved me and prayed for me every day.

She also put me back in touch with my last high school girlfriend. Patty was the daughter of one of Momma's childhood friends, and she had moved back to their hometown of Columbus, Ohio, while I was in the army. She was an upstanding woman from a good family, but she was struggling. Her husband had walked out, leaving her with two young children (Patty was five years older; we'd been seventeen and twenty-two when we dated), and she had diabetes-related health problems that made it hard to find steady work. When Momma told her I was in prison, she started writing to me, and pretty soon we were unburdening ourselves to each other. I even called her collect from a payphone when I escaped from prison because she was the closest person to me on the outside, and she seemed to accept my mistakes. Later, she admitted, she also remembered my voice. I could always win over women with my voice. When I was finally sprung in December 1979, still only twenty-one and ready for a new decade and a new start, Patty wired me a one-way bus ticket to Columbus.

Just over a year later, in March 1981, we were married. Momma and Daddy weren't too happy about that. Daddy said, "Why do you want a ready-made family?" He didn't like that Patty already had kids. Momma didn't like that either, or that Patty was full-figured, or that she didn't have the upper class breeding, the so-called *dignity*, Momma was looking for.

She said, "Why you want to tie yourself down, son? You're so young." And she didn't say it, but I heard it: *You're still my little boy.*

It was a compromise on my part, and I think Momma could sense that, too. Not a compromise with Patty, because I loved that girl. She was funny, intelligent, a good mom, an amazing cook, and I enjoyed being around her. It was a professional compromise, because I still wanted to be a radio man. I took courses at the American Broadcasting School, I sent out my résumé, but it just wasn't happening. With my prison record and lack of contacts, I couldn't get a radio job, so I looked around for a second option and thought, *Well, I'll just be a family man.* Patty and I had a child together by then, and another on the way, so it was the right thing to do.

And I was a good father because I really loved those kids. You can ask Tricia and Tangela, Patty's two kids by her ex-husband— I never treated them different. I was always Daddy to them, and I loved them like they were my own. I took them around town. I bought them treats. I played dolls and house with them. I even jumped rope and helped Patty fix their braids, because hair was a big deal to those girls. I was twenty-three years old, and I had four little daughters, and I embraced that life, tried to be the best daddy I could be, even though I wasn't around that much. I was working days as a security guard at a state-run youth detention home and picking up shifts as a security guard four or five nights a week. Despite my record, I was accepted into the cadet-in-training program of the Franklin County sheriff's department, working security at minor league baseball games and similar low-risk assignments. There were days I could see myself entering law enforcement full-time, working like my old man, retiring with a pension, a few grand-kids, and Patty at my side.

But there was another side of me, too, the Brother T side. I may have been married with kids and a few steady jobs, but I had no intention of turning into my father. I still had the dream of being Ted Williams, disc jockey. So I worked occasionally as an emcee, introducing bands at local clubs under the stage name Star. It was a scene in the early 1980s, people had a way of carrying themselves then. Soul was at its height—Marvin Gaye, big Afros, bright pants—and even in a town like Columbus, great music was coming out of the black-owned clubs. Black Is Beautiful was out, but the beauty of blackness was in, with those laid-back erotic beats that seemed to melt right into the street. We didn't have much money, but we had arrived as a people, just for a moment, and everywhere you went the radio was tuned to our station, WVKO, the only black radio station in town. That was our soundtrack, Prince and early Michael Jackson and Sugarhill Gang, Barry White for the ladies and Isaac Hayes for the players, and I loved it, *loved it*—but I couldn't help notice there were no big radio personalities anymore, like Hank Spann and Frankie Crocker. The DJs were smooth, riding under the music instead of on top of it, and to me it sounded flat.

That laid-back vocal style fit the times, though, and it certainly fit my deep, smooth voice. When they heard me talk, people in the neighborhood insisted they heard me on the radio. They called me VKO, even after they found out I wasn't on the air.

"Hey, VKO," they'd say when I walked into a bar. "When you gonna be on the radio?"

I'd grab a beer, smile, and tell them, "Maybe someday, brother, maybe someday."

I didn't tell them I'd applied to WVKO twice and been turned down. Or that I was still trying to pay off those classes at the American Broadcasting School. I just told them I was happy at the detention center, where the kids teased me about my voice even more than the brothers in the bar did. I was happy with the cadet-in-training program and my four little girls. I mean, I wasn't nobody. I was known around the neighborhood, always went to the best shows, emceed at the hot clubs, liked to have a good time. I still had my drinking problem, always had that. My oldest daughter, Tangela, who was seven, will tell you about seeing Daddy tuck a bottle of Mad Dog wine into his pocket every morning before heading off to work, and Patty will tell you about the nights I didn't make it home. We argued about that, Patty and me, but that doesn't mean I didn't love her. I respected her, that's for sure, because she was a good person. A loyal wife, a wonderful mother. And I liked the life Patty gave me: family, church, stability, kids.

We could have gone on like that, I think. We could have been happy, I think, even though I felt in my heart that I was giving up my dream.

Then, in 1984, two new stations entered the Columbus market, WZZT and WCKX. They were called urban stations back then, because they played black music by black folks for black folks. WCKX was bigger, but WZZT was hungrier to find an audience. *Hot WZZT*, they called themselves, *playing the hard-edge funk and heavier beats.* They hit the streets hard, selling advertising cheap, so a band I was friendly with, Keith Staten and the Break Your Body Band, asked me to cut a commercial for an upcoming gig. The commercial was simple: a sample of music followed by my golden voice giving the time and place. We went up to the production studio at WZZT and I nailed it on the first take. When I walked out of the booth, the station manager was waiting.

"Are you on the air?"

"Nah. Used to be, but not now."

He hired me on the spot. And not just for a Sunday countdown, like when I was in North Carolina, but for prime time, weekdays from seven P.M. to midnight.

It still gives me a chill to think about walking into that studio for the first time, opening the mike, and saying, "First in the Capital City with stereo rhythm twenty-four hours a day, we're Z103, and this is Ted Williams with you all night long." I'd put on some hot R&B, maybe Prince and the Revolution's "Let's Go Crazy," or Kurtis

Blow, and just leaned back and soaked it in. The booth, the mike, the 850,000 citizens of the greater Columbus area: This was the dream.

There were two kinds of music on urban stations then, easy listening for the ladies and the bumpity-bump for the men. I was the bumpity-bump guy, hired to play the up-tempo tracks and get the party started—so I took my people-pleasing personality onto the air, the voice I'd developed while emceeing at the clubs. I wasn't Star, though, or Brother T, no nicknames this time. I was myself, Ted Williams, the man with the voice you love by choice, just bigger and badder than I'd ever been in life.

I worked hard. I came in early every day to work on my production, recording segments and splicing them together with sound effects. When I say splicing, I mean old-school technique, taking a knife and cutting portions out of a magnetic tape, then splicing them back together in a new order and respooling them for that night's show. I eased out of the gate at seven P.M. with smooth jams, then ratcheted up the excitement hour by hour as listeners finished their dinners, put their kids to bed, and hit the dance floor. By ten o'clock, I was high-energy, man, your personal emcee, bringing the party to your living room with a voice pitched to reach ten thousand people at a time. That was the secret, to bring them all to the floor, to use my voice to make it feel like a nonstop party for a million people until 11:15, 11:30, when I slipped into a slower style, drew my words out more, allowed that sexy timbre to inundate my voice until, at two minutes to midnight, I'd slide one last record on the player and almost whisper, "The clock on the wall says it's time for me to go, brothers and sisters, but you stay right here at Z103, the hottest R&B, and we'll keep you rocking all night long."

I'd drop the needle on something soft, maybe Billy Ocean, then whisper over the opening chords, "Get ready, Patty, it's music for lovers." When I got home about one thirty, after looping spools for my next shift and cleaning up my postproduction, Patty'd be waiting with a glass of vodka, and I'd spin records on my personal stereo for another hour or two.

Man, I was proud. Proud for myself, proud for Patty, proud for my kids, who were growing up with a successful father. I got so proud, in fact, that I forgot myself: forgot where I'd come from, forgot who had given me a second chance, forgot the lessons from my first fall from grace. By the second rating period, I was number one in my time slot for young men and teens, so I jumped to WCKX as their hot new morning-drive jock. I was by far the most successful disc jockey at the station, winning the Arbitron ratings in my time slot even though our main rival, WVKO, was giving away ten thousand dollars a week, and I had nothing to give away but albums and hats.

The station didn't want me to be just a disc jockey, though; they wanted me to be a local celebrity. If there was a community event, like a parade or a picnic, I was there as "Ted Williams, the Golden Voice of WCKX." Every night, it seemed, I was at a concert or in a club, supporting the station. These were top events, where the women were beautiful and the men successful, and I was the life of the party. Like popcorn in a popper, that's how my buddy Al Battle, a local concert promoter, described me. A people pleaser, that's what I really was, a man who derived his self-esteem from the people around him, and boy did I love it. I was meeting the right people, cutting two or three radio commercials a week for several hundred dollars apiece, and it wasn't long before I really was a local celebrity.

Everywhere I went, people were handing me drinks, and I couldn't stop. I was always cordial. Always posed for a photograph and stayed to chat. I listened to every album the promoters gave me, went to every concert for every promising band. Being a disc jockey was a big deal then, and I took it seriously. We were a primary entry point into the music industry. We made our own choices about the music we played, and DJs like me could break a local band into the mainstream, or make a minor hit *the* sound of the summer. We could make a station, too, which was why management wanted us out there every night, where we could be seen as well as heard.

That was my excuse when Patty complained about all the late nights, that I was just doing my job. And it's true, I was. But I was a wet brain from the moment they stuck free drinks in my hand. I was a drunk, to put it nicely, and before long everyone in radio knew it. Too often, a good night ended with Ted Williams, radio man, passed out in his new car.

It wasn't long before I was sleeping in the production office at WCKX and rolling out of bed for my morning shift. Patty and I were on the rocks by then, mostly over my drinking. We fought for months, blistering the walls, and the more she pointed out my failings the more I resented her. I got to the point where I wasn't a husband anymore, and I wasn't much of a father either. I was never around, and when I was, I was half in the bag, stumbling in at two in the morning, cursing as I stepped on my daughters' ball-shaped braid-holders in the dark. I threw those braid-holders out every night in a fit of anger, and my daughters cried, and I felt bad, so I bought them again the next day.

Eventually, I stopped coming home. I told myself, "It's better to hurt her once, Ted, and leave her than to hurt her every night."

So I turned my back and, God help me, I never looked back. If loving the wrong woman in North Carolina was my first mistake,

leaving the right woman in Columbus, Ohio, was my second. It's
the one I've always regretted, too, because it was the moment I
turned from the righteous path. Not part of the way, like I had
before, but all the way around. It was the moment I walked out on
my good life.

Even then, I knew I was wrong. I knew, with my drinking, I was
on a bad road. That didn't stop me, though. Instead, I used it as a
justification. I told myself Patty was better off without a man who
couldn't be sober or faithful. I convinced myself Tricia, Tangela,
Julia, and even little Jenay, my youngest, only two years old, were
better off with visits than a full-time drunken dad. God help me,
but I didn't see it as a problem. I was given up by my birth mother,
after all, and God provided. No reason God couldn't provide for
my daughters, too, especially with my monthly checks.

I wanted to be free, though, and that's the real truth. I wanted
to drink when I wanted, stumble home when I wanted, date the
beautiful women that hung around at parties to hear my voice. I
wanted to live for the moment, and everything in my life reflected
it, including my radio act. Sometimes I was so hungover I barely
had the energy, but most mornings I cut loose. Forget that smooth
mellow late-1970s DJ sound. This was the swinging eighties, I was
a free man, and the wilder my life, the wilder my act—since it
wasn't an act at all, it was just Ted Williams. I had a gimmick called
Crack That Whip. Someone would call, like a kid complaining
about his momma sleeping in, and I'd hit a whip effect—
ssshhh-pow—and say, "Momma, this is Ted Williams cracking that
whip. Get up and get your little girl some breakfast." Pretty soon
women were complaining about boyfriends, and I called them out,
right on the air.

A local restaurant called J.P.'s had the slogan "We feed the people." One morning I announced: "According to the AP, and that's the Associated Press, people, J.P. has changed its name to P.J. Their new slogan: We feed the people, and now we sleep with them, too." Listeners thought that was hilarious, but J.P. pulled $35,000 in advertising from the station and demanded an apology, which the station manager personally gave over the air.

Another morning, hungover and in a foul mood, I got tired of people calling in and asking for "Lean on Me" by Club Nouveau. That's all I heard that month: "Can you play 'Lean on Me' by Club Nouveau? Can you play 'Lean on Me' by Club Nouveau?" Finally, I said, "Listen up, Columbus. Get your tape recorders ready, because here's your chance to get your own personal recording of 'Lean on Me' by Club Nouveau." Then I put the extended 12-inch version on and hit repeat. After three times, the station manager called the booth and said, "If I hear 'Lean on Me' one more time, you're fired."

I closed the door and broke the key off in the lock. "This is Ted Williams, Columbus, and this may be my last morning on air. But when I go, never say I didn't play . . . 'Lean on Me.'" I played that record for an hour before the locksmith finally drilled through the lock.

Needless to say, they fired me. But the next morning when they didn't hear my voice, black people rallied against the station. They called the switchboard, honked their horns on the street outside, even marched into the lobby of the building. So WCKX hired me back.

A few months later, I slapped the station owner's daughter at a dance club during an all-night radio promotion. She claimed I had taken too many VIP tickets for my friends, and when I didn't rise to the bait, she called me a "white thief." I was dead drunk and so was she, and if you've read this far, you probably know it wasn't "thief" that bothered me.

You also know I didn't have the humility to admit my error and take my lumps. Instead, when the station owner started yelling at me the next morning, I walked out the door, down the street, and into the offices of WVKO, the big-dog radio station of black Columbus, the one that wouldn't have hired me to be their janitor a year before.

They hired me that night and gave me the afternoon shift. It wasn't three months before I reached the top: the number one disc jockey in the greater Columbus metropolitan area.

CHAPTER 5

So that's the story of how a young boy from the projects accomplished his dream and became, at age twenty-six, Ted Williams: The Man with the Golden Voice. There were a few small bumps in the road, if you consider being kicked out of the army, spending a year in jail, and losing a marriage small bumps. Sure, there were a few lucky breaks along the way, but you make your own luck, you know? You practice and hustle, so when God opens the door, you're standing there in your best suit ready to go.

I guess I could have tried to climb a higher mountain. There were bigger places to go than the number one slot in Columbus, Ohio. I could have gone to New York City and tried to be the next Hank Spann. I could have gone into national syndication. But my sights were never set that high. I may have prayed for a million people to hear my voice, but all I wanted, really, was a microphone. It wasn't about money and it wasn't about a party. The lifestyle was more about my alcoholism than the desire to see and be seen. All I really wanted was to sit in a room and let my voice make me somebody. I wanted an identity, like Hank Spann, that I created out of air in the theater of the mind. I wanted black folks to listen and think, "Ted Williams, he's one of us."

If you know anything about my life, though, you know success isn't the end of my story. The road up was nothing compared to the road down, and during the coming years almost everyone I've mentioned in the book so far got hurt. That's the hardest part: the way I've hurt the people I've loved. The way I betrayed my family. The way I fell so far from God, and human decency, that I couldn't even hear His golden voice, the only voice that matters. I was the prodigal son, but I'm here to tell you: The world doesn't take you back, not at first.

There are a lot of reasons I fell from grace. I was selfish. I was egotistical. I wasn't grateful for what I had or the people who gave it to me. I took the shortcut when I should have worked; I left things behind when I thought I didn't need them anymore. I took my gift and left the house of the Lord, entering into the world of drunkenness and greed.

I was an alcoholic, God help me, and I can't forget that awful truth, because my failings led to more addiction, and my addictions cost me twenty years.

It was a poverty of the soul, brothers and sisters, it was a poverty of spirituality. When I was a child, I asked God for a millions ears to hear me, and God asked me back, "What will you do with them?"

I didn't hear Him. I didn't know He was asking something of me. But even if I had heard Him, I didn't have an answer.

I suppose I would have said, "I'll make them happy, Lord. I'll entertain them." That's what I was, an entertainer.

But what good was I going to do with it? At twenty-six years old, I reached a position of influence in the black community in Columbus, Ohio. I was a successful entertainer. But what good did I do with it? Did I promote charities? No, I promoted bands. Did I visit churches? No, I visited nightclubs. Did I try to address the problems in the black community? No, I made fun of them.

And then, through drug addiction, I became those problems.

I wasn't in radio for influence. I wasn't in radio for money. I was making close to six figures a year, with commercial and appearance fees, and I never bought a house. I bought a car and a stereo, a closet full of Bobby 500 suits (because I was always a formal dresser, I got that from my momma), and a nice Timex watch, but beyond that I possessed nothing of value. Most of my money went into drinks and favors for my friends, and I wasn't alone in that sin. Lots of radio people from those days became addicts like me.

I never planned to give back. I never thought of radio as a way to do good or spread a positive message. I was in the game for the fame, and I was into the fame for the self-respect. I wanted to be recognized. I wanted black kids to say when I walked down the street *That's Ted Williams. I want to be like Ted Williams when I grow up.* I wanted black women to say *I wish my man had more Ted Williams in him,* and for the black men to say *Ted Williams, dang, that Negro's got balls to the floor.*

I stayed in touch with Patty. I saw my children once a week, and I gave them gifts and money when I could. But I didn't want that quiet lifestyle. I didn't want my father's life. The world was buzzing, and it was there for me to take. These were the golden years, before people knew about AIDS and before drugs devastated the black community. I mean, we saw stories about crack on the television, but that was Los Angeles and New York, that was some other black world. In Columbus, it was still cocaine, mountains of it, and you still heard Luther Vandross seducing women on the radio rather than N.W.A. The clubs were packed with girls, and everybody wanted a good time. I didn't have any interest in cocaine. For me, it was alcohol, just alcohol and women. I could have slept my way around Columbus because I had the voice, and women would melt when I opened my mouth. They might give the cold shoulder to my Lionel Richie Jheri curl, but as soon as I said *Hi, baby, Ted Williams. Who are you?* their eyes opened wide, the coldness dropped from their shoulders, and pretty soon we'd be bent over our cocktails, talking low.

But that wasn't for me. No matter where I've been, whether high or low—or lying low—I've always been a one-woman man. Oh, I cheated, don't get me wrong, I've taken my opportunities, and I'm not proud of that. But I was loyal in my way. I let women into my heart. I cared for them. Except for Patty, I've never walked away from a woman I loved. They've always been the ones to walk away from me.

And the woman for me, once I walked away from my life with Patty, was Lisa, lovely Lisa. What can I say about Lisa? I'd like to say it was her mind that attracted me, or even her personality, but I can't think about Lisa without thinking of her beauty: light skin, round hips, radiant smile. She was young and fresh, the girl of my dreams, and better yet, the girl of every man's dreams.

Lisa and I were made for each other, I suppose, but not by God, because I had turned away from Him. I had turned my back on the good life, but I was hanging on, just barely, to the man Patty had wanted me to be. Once I met Lisa, though, I started to forget myself. I forgot to visit my children, I forgot to return Patty's calls. I started spending money on jewelry instead of hair braids.

My parents came to town, and I was too busy working and partying to see them. Instead, I called their motel room and said, "Momma, turn on the radio."

I waited for her to dial in, then opened the mike and said, "Good morning, Columbus, and a fine good morning to my parents, Al-fred and Julia Williams, who are visiting from Brooklyn, New York. I love you both."

When I closed the mike and picked up the phone, Momma said simply, "That's nice."

She was happy for me. She knew I was living my dream, the only thing I'd wanted since I was ten years old. She was a great momma, she wanted me to be happy, but she didn't understand why radio meant so much to me, or why I wanted so badly to be heard. She didn't understand why I'd left behind a family, when all she'd ever wanted was children of her own.

My father understood. My father saw that his boy, the one he'd written off, was a success. He heard my voice on the radio, he saw the posters with my picture on them, and more important, he saw Lisa. My father never liked Patty—funny, isn't it, that he would dislike the one woman who was good for me? Patty was dark, and he always said a dark-skinned girl was an anchor to her man.

But he loved light-skinned Lisa, because they were alike. They were both high-steppers and stylish dressers (nobody wore a nice dress better than Lisa), and they were both color-struck. I've never met two people that cared more about the color of someone's skin. I sent them out together while I worked, on the Ted Williams tab of course, and they talked and laughed all day, drank and danced away the afternoon. I joined them that night in the VIP section of the O'Jays concert, because my father loved the O'Jays, and when the night was over, I had him. I had my father. For a moment there I could see it, the greatest irony of all: My father didn't want the Al Williams life either. He really wanted to be like me.

Only twice in my adult life was my father proud of me. The first was my graduation from army basic training. The second was that day in Columbus, when he could no longer deny his boy done good.

No, his boy had done better. Better than his old man. The radio gig, the VIP concert tickets, and especially Lisa, lovely Lisa. That girl was *his* dream, because whenever she walked into a room, she *was* the room. He was proud of me for having her. He was *proud*, and I loved him for it. And I loved Lisa for it, too. She was the ultimate sign of my success.

I was hooked on her, that's for sure, especially after my father's visit. I put her on a pedestal, in the place where God should have been, and I worshipped her. We went to every party together. We drank vodka in her apartment together. I gave her clothes and shoes and anything she wanted, including a famous man to hang on her arm. And we had fun. She could drink and dance and drive you crazy, absolutely crazy in bed, and what more could a man want?

For two years, it was a wonderful ride. Everywhere I went, it was free food, free drinks, free merchandise and tickets. I was emceeing concerts for Morris Day, Con Funk Shun, the Ohio Players, the Gap Band. I dropped in backstage any time I wanted. Every promoter in Columbus knew that if you wanted black people at your event, you wanted Ted Williams, so I was constantly on call. But they also knew Ted Williams meant a good time. During the day, I voiced commercials, touted bands, gave interviews, and afterward, there was always another concert, another station event, another after-party to attend.

I was tiptop, brother. Tiptop. I mean, there were T-shirts with my picture on them, and people were wearing them, too. The station handed out thousands of business cards with my name and picture on them. There were so many of them I'd find them on the sidewalk. It was common for me to hit the button for the advertising block and for all three commercials to feature my voice. I even did a hilarious old-man voice for Southeast Seafood, one of my

regular sponsors. Why Southeast Seafood would want an old Jew-
ish man to hawk their fish instead of the Golden Voice, I don't
know, but I loved doing it, loved wearing the headphones in the
booth and hearing myself say, "Hey, you there, Southeast Seafood
has the best prices on fresh fish. They've got the catfish on special
this week, $2.99 a pound, so come on down."

In 1987, I was recruited for a drive-time job in Cleveland, a big
promotion to a major market. By then, my drinking was out of
control. I'd wake up in the morning and drink vodka, or if I didn't
have any vodka, I'd buy a bottle of Mad Dog 20/20 Orange Jubilee,
the orange juice of the alcoholic, on the way to the station. I drank
in the booth, even taking a sip now and then on the air. I fought
with Lisa because her ex-husband, the father of her children, was
out of prison, and she was seeing him again, too.

So I left the mess behind. Said good-bye to my kids, dumped
Lisa, and bought a ticket to a new life in Cleveland. I was sitting on
the Greyhound bus, five minutes from departure, when Lisa ran
up, begging for forgiveness. She'd left her other man, she told me.
She wanted to be with me. I took her back. What else could I do? I
loved her.

Patty said, when she heard we were back together, "She's gonna
get pregnant, Ted. She's gonna get pregnant, and that's going to be
the end of us."

And that's exactly what happened. By that winter, Lisa was
pregnant. A few months later, I went back to Columbus to attend
a WCKX concert and fell into a blackout drunk. For three days I
didn't call anybody, and nobody knew where I was. By the time I
got back to Cleveland, I'd been demoted. Obviously, there were
other issues. My drinking was worse than ever, the station knew I
had problems, and I remember thinking, during my first midday

shift, that Cleveland wasn't going to work out. Lisa didn't want to
stay anyway, so I quit, took back my morning drive shift on WCKX,
and moved into Lisa's apartment in the north end of Columbus,
which she'd never even bothered to give up.

A few months later, on August 16, 1988, my son Desmond was
born. I was thirty years old. I remember marveling at his tiny smile,
those innocent hands, that caramel beauty like his mother. I must
have prayed to God, thanking Him for my miracle, but I don't remember the prayer. I just remember four friends coming down from Cleveland to celebrate. We were in my tiny living room, with the lights low
and the stereo thrumming soft enough that it wouldn't wake three-
day-old Desmond, who was in his bassinet in the corner, sound asleep.
I had a habit by then; I drank until I started falling down and crashing
into things, then I smoked a marijuana joint to take the edge off. So I
didn't think anything of it when, after a bottle of vodka or two, my
friend rolled a joint, took a hit, and handed it to me.

When I hit it, though, something wasn't right. I tasted mint, like
a York Peppermint Pattie, and my hair follicles came alive. I started
to sweat in the armpits, but it wasn't a bad thing, it was an adrena-
line rush, an energy that seemed to lift me off the floor. Usually
when I smoked pot, I got a dull feeling, like cotton in my head, but
this time I wasn't tired. I didn't get paranoid or want to sleep. I heard
the music, I saw the lights, and I liked it. I really, really liked it.

"What's with that weed?" I asked.

"Got some rock in it, man," my friend said, rolling.

I knew rock was cocaine. I'd never used cocaine, but it had been
around the scene forever, so it didn't seem like a big deal to push
myself forward one time, reach out my hand, and say, "Well if that's
how cocaine feels, then let me have one more."

CHAPTER 6

can't tell you why crack is so addictive. It's just cocaine, cooked up with baking soda until it becomes a rocklike substance. Drop a piece of crack on a glass table and the sound pops, like a marble, because crack is hard. You take a rock, bust it into pieces, and that's how you smoke it. Sometimes the rock is yellow, the best variety back in the day. Other times it's white, known as "tight white," ultimately my favorite kind. The bag my friends left me when they went back to Cleveland held about eight pieces of the yellow, about the size of a penny each, so I crumbled one up every night and put it on a joint (a pri-mo). Lisa didn't smoke the first night, but I pressured her, and she sprinkled a little in her cigarette the second night (a cig-mo), and she liked it almost as much as I did.

And that's the problem: I liked it. I liked it a lot. I loved the mint taste in my mouth and I loved the way it made me feel. Not euphoric, but energetic, like I could tackle the world. It made me feel good about myself. Lots of guys want sex on crack because the drug opens your sensory receptors, but I was never like that. Most of the time, especially in those first weeks, Lisa and I just sat and stared at the door because the high was so intense, and staring at that door felt like fun.

But the high lasted only ten minutes, and then I had to break up another rock, or hunt for more, because after where I'd been, the real world was awful, just awful, and I wanted to get back to staring at the door.

I thought, *I can just smoke on the weekends.*

Then, *I can just smoke at night and every weekend, and everything will be fine.*

I said to myself, *Crack's good for me because it keeps me off alcohol. Crack's gonna save my life.*

There wasn't any question of wanting more, so after a few days I went down to my old neighborhood on the east side of Columbus, where I knew a lot of people, and started looking for a dealer. This was 1988, crack was raging on the coasts but it was just getting a foothold in Ohio, and it took me a minute to find a brother who dealt rock. I bought a twenty-dollar piece—three to four hits, depending on how you broke it up—and flaked up the whole thing on one joint (a stackie). A couple hours later, I was back for more, and that brother became my regular dealer.

Within a week he was waiting for me outside the radio station. I had my show down to a science by then. The first hour and a half, 6:00 A.M. to 7:30 A.M., was high energy, the Golden Voice getting people out of bed, making them laugh, starting their day light and bright. The next hour was mostly information, the headlines, the traffic and the weather, with a little humor thrown in. By 9:00 A.M., most of my listeners were in school or at work, so I brought my voice down low and slow, played more music, eased them into their day, and then, over the last half hour, into the disc jockey on the midday shift. By 11:00 A.M., I was out the door, and my dealer was around the corner. I'd slip him a few bucks and a stolen CD, and then there was nothing to do for the rest of the day but smoke.

Even that wasn't enough. I smoked my first hit on August 20, 1988. By mid-September my dealer was visiting me in the booth, and my radio shifts were blown apart. Light and bright? Smooth and mellow? I didn't care about that anymore. All I wanted was to get off the air as quickly as possible. Lisa was waiting for me at home, and we'd smoke stackies all afternoon and stare at the door, impossibly happy but increasingly paranoid, because crack heightens your senses, especially your hearing, and we never knew what was beyond the door.

I discovered the pipe a few weeks later. I was at my dealer's buying a rock, and one of his friends pulled out a pipe and said, "You ever try this?"

"Nah," I said, not thinking anything of it.

But when I saw that smoke gathering in the glass stem, I got hungry. Real hungry. The smoke looked so thick and luscious, I could almost taste it. So I asked for a hit. I smoked the next rock and I was hooked, absolutely hooked. It was so powerful. The crack exploded in my head and then it went shooting through my bloodstream, straight out to the ends of my fingers and toes, and I felt alive, I felt like I never wanted to be anywhere but curled up in the pipe.

I took it home. A few days later, with my head blown off with crack, I asked Lisa, "Do you love me because I'm on radio, or do you love me because of who I am?"

"I love you for who you are, baby."

"Then I'm quitting my job and we'll smoke all day."

So I walked out. Two months after smoking my first hit of crack, I walked out on my dream job, the only thing I'd ever wanted to do with my life.

I wasn't any good by then anyway. I was missing shifts. I was ignoring phone calls. I had a beeper, and I'd shake like a leaf when that thing went off because I was bent over the crack pipe, and I knew it was the production manager trying to find me. My crack dealer was coming into the station, sometimes two or three times a shift. I was smoking on the air, and that's not a good idea with a drug as strong as crack. I'd take a hit and forget to open the mike after a song, or I'd play ten songs in a row just to listen to them spin. When I wasn't high, I was obsessed with getting out of the booth and getting high, or I was staring at the clock wondering when my boy was coming by.

Without the job, though, things fell apart. Lisa and I did nothing but smoke and look at the door, paranoid out of our minds. Desmond was in his bassinet, two months old, but most of the time we didn't have the energy to rock him. I was constantly hungry, constantly looking for crack, and every white speck on our floor had to be investigated, in case it was a flake I'd lost. I burned a lot of cat litter that way, until the cat disappeared. When it turned icy in November, the rock salt from the front walk made me crazy, because it got on the carpet and looked like rock, but when I put it on the pipe it sizzled and smoked and I knew it was nothing. Once or twice I tried to smoke it anyway because I was that desperate, that deep in the drug. One night I saw a red glow at the window and I was sure it was the devil himself, coming to take me to hell, but I kept smoking and blasting, smoking and blasting, thinking, *Just give me one more hit before I go, just one more hit.* About ten hits later the fire engine showed up, and that's when I realized the house across the street was engulfed in flames. They found the owner lying against the front door, burned beyond recognition.

If that isn't a metaphor for crack, I don't know what is, because by Thanksgiving I was hocking the furniture. Within three months of my first smoke, most of what I'd accumulated in my five years at the top was gone: the couch, the dining room table, my watch, Lisa's jewelry, Desmond's bassinet. I'd lost all my old friends, unless I'd hooked them on crack, too, because I was an advocate for the stuff, I was telling everyone how great it was. Then when they wanted to come over and smoke, I charged them a "tax," meaning they had to give us a hit of crack to get in the door. After a while, we had a whole new set of friends. Desmond would be sleeping upstairs and we'd have three or four tax-paying crackheads, people I barely knew, smoking in our living room. They were coming by at all hours, waking Desmond, eating our food (until we stopped buying food), sleeping on our floor—and it was no secret to the neighbors that our apartment was no longer the home of a radio announcer with a nice family, but a gateway to hell.

By then, I was stealing. My dealer loved CDs, he always wanted the latest music, so when I quit the radio station I didn't go quietly, I cleaned out the CD room. That meant I could never go back to a radio station. Word was out about Ted Williams, so shoplifting became a primary means of supporting my habit.

Another was commercials. I'd made a lot of business contacts over the years, so for a while I made money cutting radio spots for local music clubs and pawnshops. When I said "Hello, Columbus. This is Ted Williams for U.S.A. Pawn," there was still magic in my voice, people still wanted to buy what I was selling. But as soon as I touched the money, I was gone. I wasn't hanging out with the production managers anymore, wasn't going to the clubs to listen to the bands. I was in a dope apartment, paying my own "tax" to smoke, or I was home with Lisa, where we could smoke two hundred dollars, my average paycheck for a fifteen-second commercial, in less than a day.

So I started hitting up business contacts for loans and extra cash until finally it was them, not me, ducking out after our recording sessions. I was hitting up friends, too—those who were left. And especially my momma.

I told Momma I was out of work and needed money for the electric bill. I told her I had a baby and he needed to be fed. My father said, "Get a job," and slammed down the phone, but Momma always came through. She kept us going for months, especially after Lisa became pregnant with our second child, because Momma couldn't turn her back on a pregnant woman and another grandbaby on the way.

We lost our apartment anyway, in February 1989. A month later, we were arrested in Lazarus department store. Lisa and I had a scam where we'd grab clothes off hangers, then take them back to the counter for a refund. The refund was store credit, but if you took that credit to another department and bought something small, they'd give you the change in cash. We worked that scam for a few weeks at different department stores until one day Lisa made the exchange for the cash and, while coming down the escalator toward the exit, reached over and grabbed a scarf.

I was standing at the door waiting for her, so I could see the two undercover security guards following her. I tried to signal her to put the scarf back, but she stuffed it in her bag and kept walking toward me. One of the security guards reached to grab her as she neared the exit. I knew she was caught, and without thinking, I jumped in and knocked him down. Suddenly, we were all struggling and fighting each other, with Lisa pregnant, and God help me I never thought about her or the baby, I just knew she had money in her purse, and I needed that money to see me through the next couple of days. If the opportunity presented itself, I'd have grabbed her purse and run straight to the crack house, leaving her behind.

In the end, the courts knocked the charge down from robbery to theft, and Lisa got eighteen months. Halfway through her sentence, on a date in late 1989 I can't even recall, they brought her from the Ohio Reformatory for Women in Marysville to the Ohio State University Hospital, where she delivered our son Tyrell in a guarded room. I picked Tyrell up, walked out of the hospital, took the bus to my aunt's house, and left him there.

CHAPTER 7

I got my first Ohio prison number in 1990 for my part in the department store theft. (It was Pen #219336, for all you lottery players.) My sentence was deferred a year, so I went in the week before Lisa was released. I served four months, compared to the year Lisa served on her eighteen-month sentence. By the time I got out, Lisa had Tyrell back from my aunt and Desmond back from my momma, who had taken him back to Brooklyn while Lisa was in jail. Desmond was the hard one, because Momma didn't want to give him back. She loved that boy. And she was disgusted by Lisa. She wasn't happy with me, but I was her son—and a man. She'd never known a man to care about kids. But for a mom to turn her back on her children for a drug? That wasn't something Momma could understand.

But Lisa was clean, she was living in an apartment across the street from her grandmother's house, so Momma had no choice. I still remember the way Desmond ran to me the day I got out of prison, the way he hugged me and smiled the biggest smile in the world. I'd lost my four girls by then, the ones I'd raised with Patty. I had taken Jenay to the park one day, and instead of playing with her, I slipped away and smoked crack. Jenay saw me and started crying. She wouldn't stop crying all day, but I wouldn't stop smoking, and she must have told Patty because I wasn't welcome back after that.

So little Desmond, who loved me so much, should have been my salvation. Tyrell was too small, he was just a baby, but Desmond . . . he was my little man, always followed at his daddy's heel, always thought the world of me. He smiled every time I talked to him because he was starved for attention, and he wanted a daddy so bad. No matter what I did, that little boy idolized me.

But as soon as I put him to bed that first night, I turned to Lisa and said, "You thinking about getting high?"

"I sure am," she said. She wasn't cured, far from it—she was an addict like me. An hour later, we were bent over the crack pipe in our living room while my three-year-old "little man" watched over his baby brother upstairs.

It didn't have to be like that. I still had friends from the old days who wanted to help me. I wasn't too far out of the game. They'd see me on the street, since I lived less than a mile from WCKX, and say, "What's the matter with you, Ted? Get yourself cleaned up and back on the radio." There was still a door open, despite my past. If I'd gone back with an honest heart, admitted my mistakes, and asked for another chance, dope-free, they'd have given it to me.

But I couldn't do it. Even with Desmond's love, I didn't have the heart to quit. Even as I was putting him to bed I was thinking, *Go to sleep now, just go the hell to sleep,* because I was dreaming about the pipe. There's a ritual to packing a hit of crack, and that ritual ran in my mind like a movie, consuming my thoughts, even as I was tucking in my little man. Break a penny-size rock into two pieces. Ball the "chore"—a piece of steel mesh torn off a Brillo or Chore

Boy scouring pad. Shove it into the end of the pipe. Place the rock on the chore. Hold the lighter to the rock. Watch it glow. Watch it start to bubble. Put the pipe to your lips. Inhale through the flame. Hold it. Hold it. Blow.

I didn't care about my family. I didn't care about radio. I wasn't intimidated by the things I'd need to do to get back on the air: clean up, apologize, reconnect with friends, humble myself, start small. I didn't even think about those things, because all I could think about was the rock glowing on the chore, and the smoke rushing down the pipe. Radio, family, I couldn't see it. I couldn't see any other life, because crack obscured it all.

I was a broken man, morally and psychologically, but prison didn't break me. Prison inspired me, because I was a celebrity inside. WCKX broadcasted out of London, Ohio, where the prison was located, and a lot of inmates remembered my voice. They even remembered my act, especially Crack That Whip. Those boys fell out when I did my old routines, making up new characters as I went along. I suppose that was sad, living among men who used to write letters asking me to dedicate songs to their wives and girlfriends, but I didn't feel that way. I told myself I'd quit, I'd go back to the air, but I knew it was a lie, because every night, when I lay down in my bunk to dream, I dreamt about crack.

And yet, the first hit . . . that first hit of crack on the outside . . . it broke my heart. It always does, friends, it always does. The first hit after a long hiatus is nothing but shame, because it's the moment when you realize, even as you hunger for that blast, that there's no change, not this time, Lord, not this time.

The old life came on me so fast, I didn't even have time to contemplate a straight life. I don't have any memories, outside of those first moments with Desmond, of being straight. Lisa and I went right back to living the way we already had: smoking, stealing, hitting up my momma for money. We went on welfare. We accepted food stamps. Lisa even, at one point, started dating dealers. This was the woman I loved, the one woman I put on a pedestal and worshipped before God, and I didn't try to stop her. In fact, I encouraged her, because those relationships meant crack, and crack meant more to me than Lisa, meant more to me at that point than anything—and it wasn't even close.

It took four months, I think, to lose our apartment, because Momma paid one month and the eviction notice took three more. But the shame of that short time, the depths to which we fell. I remember Desmond bumping into Lisa when she was smoking, because he was always underfoot, and Lisa accidentally knocking him backward into a chair. Desmond came up with a mouth full of blood. Instead of immediately rushing to his aid, Lisa and I started arguing.

"You should take care of him. You're the one who bumped him."

"Well, you're his daddy. You're the one he ran to." This was true, Desmond ran right to his beloved Daddy, begging for a hug, but Daddy was too wrapped up in his pipe.

In the end, I stuffed a towel in his mouth and went right on smoking.

Baby Tyrell? We fed him mostly sugar water, until one day he tore off his diaper, threw it at Lisa, then rifled the bottle at her head. He didn't just throw it down, he tried to take her head off, that's how hungry the poor baby was.

It made an impression. The next time we got our food stamps, we took them straight to the store. We loaded up the cart with $200 worth of groceries, even opened the bologna and let Desmond eat it in the grocery cart. We were so proud of ourselves for feeding our kids. But when we got home, there was a drug dealer sitting on our stoop.

"Tight white," he said. "I got tight white."

We went inside and unloaded the groceries. Lisa started cooking pork chops for dinner. We were quiet, so quiet, because we were both trying not to think of it, the taste of that tight white. Finally, I couldn't take it anymore. I went back to each shelf and gathered up the groceries. Three-year-old Desmond was sitting in the living room with a bunch of grapes, watching me, and he started shoving the grapes in his mouth as fast as he could, because he knew Daddy was coming to take them away. I left him the grapes and the half-eaten bologna packet, but I returned the rest of the groceries to the store and spent the money on crack. Lisa and I smoked our brains out, until eventually I said, "We should eat those pork chops you cooked."

We went in the kitchen, and they were covered with mold. I mean, those chops were hairy; that's how long we'd left them on the cold stove.

By the time the sheriff came to kick us out, I was back in jail for parole violation. They threw my possessions out onto the street— my childhood photos, my army uniform, those business cards with Ted Williams's face on the front that WCKX used to pass out by the thousands—and by the time I made bail, with money Momma wired to Lisa, they were gone.

We kept asking Momma for electric bill money anyway. We kept asking her for rent. I kept getting arrested, but Lisa didn't ask for bail money because Momma wouldn't hear it. "Let him stay in jail," she said. "Maybe it will straighten him out." So Lisa asked for "food" money instead.

By the time my parents came to town in 1991, Momma knew we

were in trouble. She had a lot of relatives in the Columbus area, and they always called to give her the latest gossip. "Ted's not on the air anymore." "Ted was in *The Blotter* again." *The Blotter* was a local newspaper that printed police reports and arrests.

I lied to her, said I was looking for work, and I got mad when she confronted me. "Why do you believe them instead of me, Momma? I'm your son!" It didn't matter to me that I was telling lies. I needed that crack money, and crack was the only thing that mattered.

So when Momma and Daddy came to town, Lisa and I put on our best outfits. We dressed the kids in their best clothes. We dropped them off at my aunt's house, and then we went to the state fair. My momma loved the Ohio State Fair, it was her happiest childhood memory. So we rode the rides, ate hot dogs and frog legs, looked at the goofy cakes and the award-winning pies. Lisa was her old self, looking fine and talking up my father, who clearly still had a thing for her. I played the good son. It was a sad reenactment of the visit only five years before, when Lisa and I had impressed my father. The only time Al Williams had been proud of me.

This time, I didn't care what my father thought of me. The only thing I cared about was money. That's why I dressed up. That's why I tried so hard to act right. When the evening ended, I kissed my momma (the last time for twenty years, but I didn't know that then), soaked her for one hundred dollars, and asked her to drop Lisa and me off in front of our house.

Except it wasn't our house. It was a crack house. And we went straight inside and smoked every penny.

Not long after, Momma stopped wiring us money. "I've given you my last dollar, Teddy," she told me. "I don't have any more."

I thought at the time that was true, because my parents were not rich, and she had sent me thousands of dollars over the years, but apparently she got a phone call in the middle of the night from a stranger. He said, "Don't send no more baby clothes, Mrs. Williams. Your grandchildren aren't getting them. Your son's selling them for crack."

The man hung up without another word, leaving my mother scared and confused—*Crack, no way Ted's on that stuff*—and thinking about that now, I wonder if it even happened that way, or if it was her subconscious mind acknowledging, finally, what her heart already knew.

By then, Lisa and I were regulars of the Interfaith Hospitality Network, a last-chance charity for parents on their way to the street. We met every Saturday, and they'd either put us up in a donated motel room or at a church for the coming week. During the day we stayed at a family shelter, feeding our kids cereal or letting them run around with the other kids until lunchtime, when we'd trek down to the corners where the charities gave out food. We were getting three meals for the kids that way, and we had a place to stay. I remember happy moments throwing the ball in a church gym with Desmond and holding hands with my boys as we walked to the corner for food. It was a good time. There was some genuine family togetherness then. But Lisa and I were still getting high, so that wasn't going to last. Many days we'd buy a fifty-dollar hit right before getting on the bus to a church, and we'd smoke the whole rock in that church during the night.

Needless to say, we failed the charity's mandatory drug tests and, after a few warnings, were kicked out of the program. The state started the process of taking our children away, and no matter how hard Lisa fought for them it wasn't enough, because she couldn't stay clean; couldn't find a job; couldn't pass drug tests; couldn't show any proof she was making a change.

Finally, with no hope left, I called my ex-wife, Patty, and asked her to take my children. She took Desmond and she convinced my cousin to take Tyrell, because he didn't have a child of his own. There was a newspaper article when I got famous that called Patty the hero of the story, and that's true. Except for those first years, I didn't visit Patty or my daughters. I didn't know where my girls went to school; I didn't know the names of their friends; I never spent one minute helping them with their homework or talking with them about right and wrong. Patty could have hated me for that. She could have hated me for the money I never gave her or the emotional support I couldn't be bothered to provide.

But she didn't. She pitied me. She prayed for me. And she found homes for my kids, because she didn't want to see them suffer in foster care. She was Julia Williams thirty years later, holding together the fabric of the neighborhood, caring for five children with love and dedication, including one that wasn't her own—that was, in fact, the son of the woman her husband left her for. And as I'd always been for my momma, I was nothing but trouble. I popped back into Patty's life every once in a while, but only to break promises and my children's hearts. I even falsely accused my cousin of abusing Tyrell, just because the man was gay. I was so deep into the pipe that, I had lost touch with the real world, and I didn't have any idea of right or wrong.

Without Desmond and Tyrell, our lives fell apart. Those kids were the one thing that kept us pushing, kept us working toward a glimmer of sobriety and responsibility. Without them, our relationship died. Lisa changed. She didn't get off the pipe, but she started to hate and blame me. "You weren't man enough to save our children," she would scream at me. "You weren't man enough to get me a place to live. You weren't man enough to get me clean. You aren't man enough for me. All you're man enough for is crack, and that ain't no man at all."

Eventually, she kicked me out. We were living with her aunt, a good Christian woman, and Lisa told me she was going clean. It was true, but I didn't believe her. She had a check coming—I can't even remember what for—and I was convinced she wanted me out so she could smoke all the money herself. That sent me into a rage, and for the first time in my life I attacked someone in anger. I'd never been a violent person, but that morning I grabbed Lisa by the hair and yanked her to the ground. I would have choked the life out of her, I think, if her cousins hadn't jumped on top of me, because that's how mad I was for crack. I was still raging when they threw me out: raging for the crack I imagined her smoking without me, but also for my old life, when Lisa had been my obsession, my sin of choice, and not the only thing left.

But she was gone. And when that door slammed that cold morning in early 1993, I really was alone. And Godless. And lost.

CHAPTER 8

walked to a homeless shelter. I didn't know what else to do. I checked myself in, took a bed on the second floor, and thought about my life.

Then I called my momma and apologized. No scam. I didn't ask for money, I just told her where I was. She was appalled. I could hear it in her voice. For months she had started every conversation with "Are you working, son?" Every time I said no, it put a dent in her heart, but when I told her, "Momma, I'm at the homeless shelter, I got no place to live," it took her breath away. A crushing shame, that's what she felt. For a full ten seconds, she couldn't speak. I had messed up plenty, but . . . homeless. I know she felt sorry for me. She felt sorry for me my whole life, ever since my mother abandoned me. But at that moment, she felt sorrier for herself.

The homeless shelter didn't bother me, though. Momma didn't realize it because I'd been lying to her, but the place wasn't much different from how I'd been living for the past two years. And it certainly wasn't any worse than prison, where I'd already been three or four times for petty theft and parole violations. Every step down is a chance at a new beginning, though, and I embraced the shelter as a new start in life. Would it make sense if I said the shelter felt like a marriage? It was a partnership, and I dove into it headlong.

I was lucky. I didn't know anything about shelter culture, but I ended up at one of the best in Columbus—Friends of the Homeless. From the outside, Friends of the Homeless isn't much: a red-brick building surrounded by a high chain-link fence in the tough Main Street neighborhood east of downtown. Main Street was a typical inner city black area, with old row houses and a gorgeous AME church, but blighted on the very same blocks by boarded-up buildings and vacant storefronts. These days the area has been gentrified, and there are white businesses only a few blocks from the shelter, but in 1993 the only businesses were the dope houses, and I was the whitest person in the hood. That's no joke. You were a hard white-boy if you ventured down to Champion and Main in 1993.

The neighborhood wasn't why Friends of the Homeless was surrounded by the fence, though. There was a police station next door, and besides, who was going to rob a homeless shelter? The fence was to keep the dope dealers out. The gate was open during the day; in fact, like most shelters, you weren't allowed inside in the afternoon. That's when the staff ate lunch and cleaned the place, although with its decades-old linoleum and cinder block walls, Friends of the Homeless never looked or felt too clean. But there were always fresh linens and soap; nobody crapped in the shower; and the staff seemed to care. That's the most important part of a homeless shelter: the staff. If the people who work there care about the people who live there, you have a healing situation, no matter how shabby the walls. But a caring staff is rare in the shelter world.

Most of the time, the staff is just cashing checks. I've seen employees stand aside to allow a beating, and I've seen employees rob homeless people blind. At Friends of the Homeless, you could trust the staff. You could leave a bag in your storage locker without worrying about it being gone.

Even better, they offered a sober living program called Solutions and Possibilities. This was 1993, and crack was a full-blown epidemic. If you weren't there, you can't fathom how badly that drug blighted black America. My parents, their parents before them, maybe even their parents before them, those Negroes built a world. They marched; they worked under the bigot's thumb; they fixed their ghettoes with corner shops and well-tended lawns. And in a few years, crack wiped it out. Broke the windows, abandoned the buildings, put parents on the streets and twelve-year-old kids on the corners with guns, and wiped the whole thing out. There were two hundred homeless men and women in Friends of the Homeless in 1993, and I don't think there was a single one—not one—that wasn't a crack addict.

So SNP, as we called the program, was founded for rehabilitation. Take one person, turn them around, turn around the neighborhood. Believe the homeless are people and that addiction is an illness, and find a cure. The program was only a couple of months old, and it lasted only a few years, until rehabilitation of the homeless—especially crackheads—fell out of favor and the funds ran out. But while it lasted, it was a God-send to men like me, and I embraced it hard.

For the first time since leaving radio, I had a daily routine. Every day I woke up at the same time. I ate breakfast. I swept and scrubbed the second floor, where I lived, because everyone in the program had a job, and that was mine. I worked with counselors brought in to support our sobriety. There was no treatment as such, but I never missed the lunchtime Narcotics Anonymous meeting at Club Surrender, which was just down the block. I didn't work the twelve steps, and I never spoke more than to say "My name's Ted. I'm a crack addict and an alcoholic, and I'm seven days sober," but I embraced the atmosphere of the place, the hugging and anonymous faces, the strong coffee, and the humility of sweeping up cigarette butts at the end of every meeting with a push broom.

I had been raised Baptist with a little Jehovah's Witness thrown in, and at Club Surrender I found my way back to my Higher Power, the God of my understanding. He wasn't new to me, because I'd felt Him many times before. Embracing God felt like a journey home, and as I got sober I prayed for His help and understanding, and the more I prayed the better I felt about my recovery. Just open your heart and it's there, that's what I've learned over the years. Just ask.

With my two-week coin in my hand (meaning two weeks sober), I began to proselytize. I'd walk into the commons room at Friends of the Homeless every day at five minutes to twelve. There was always a big crowd waiting for the church van to arrive with lunch, so I'd unplug the television to loud groans and say, "My name's Ted, and there's a Narcotics Anonymous meeting in five minutes at Club Surrender, just down the street. It's a better way of life, brothers and sisters, and I encourage you to attend. I'm going there right now, if anybody wants to join me."

At first, people were angry. "Shut up, Ted," they yelled. "You know you still smoke."

But they were just being haters, because I was clean, I was sincere, and after a few weeks they started to tolerate my interruptions. Nothing they could do about it anyway; they knew I was

coming every day at the same time with the same invitation, because it was part of my routine, and routine keeps you clean.

I remember one middle-aged man, kind of heavy, sat right in
front of the television every day, with his arms crossed. He never
said a word, just rolled his eyes at me, and I thought, *If I can reach
that man, I've done it. I've atoned for a few of my sins.*

But day after day, the man sat quietly, until I said, "I'm going
now. Thank you for your time." Then he rose up, walked to the
television, and turned it back on.

Understand, now, that my little speech wasn't like any I'd made
before. I didn't use my radio voice. I didn't try to entertain. I wasn't
popcorn in a popper like I'd been with nightclub crowds. I just
stood there, quietly, looking at the floor for the first couple of
weeks, until I found courage in conviction, and then I looked them
in the eye. Sure, they laughed at me, but as I came back, day after
day, then week after week, people started to believe. They saw my
persistence. They saw I was making an effort. And they saw the
change. I looked healthier. I sounded better. I was friendly. I was
the old Ted Williams, the man who smiles. I was always hugging
the staff and the other residents, always trying to get them to talk
about their day.

With my thirty-day coin, I felt the shame lifting.

With my three-month coin, I got a job at Kentucky Fried
Chicken, so I had change in my pocket and another place to be
every day.

At twelve weeks, the shelter gave me a fifty-dollar gift card to
Meijer's, a local grocery store, for being such a good role model. If
SNP had a poster, I would have been on it.

By the end of the year, I was close to my six-month coin. A
woman in the shelter had gotten sober the same day as me and we

talked about it all the time. Six months. Half a year without drugs. That was a big deal. I remember walking into the television room that morning with a smile on my face, giving my same speech, watching that same man sit with his arms folded and his lips pursed. *Today is the day*, I thought. *Ted Williams is gonna be free.*

A woman decided to go with me to Club Surrender. She'd been watching me for months, and she wanted what I'd achieved. We walked out of that dim room together, out into the sunlight, and we were halfway to the meeting when I felt the seventy dollars in my pocket and a thought jumped into my head. I turned to her in that instant and said, "If I told you I had money, would you know where to get a twenty?"

She smiled because she thought I was joking.

Then she saw the hunger in my eyes, and I saw her eyes get wide with excitement, and she grabbed my hand and said, "Yes, Ted. Yes, I do."

We walked a few blocks to the crack house, and I bought a twenty-dollar rock. I can't even say what I was thinking. My mind was a blank. I had been obsessed with crack for weeks, that's my only explanation. As my six-month date neared, I thought about it more and more, and the more I thought about *not* smoking crack, the closer it came until suddenly, on that street, the thought of it—no, the very taste of it—overwhelmed me, and the words popped out of my mouth.

Ten minutes later I was in a dark room with the rock in my hand. But I didn't have a lighter. This is a crack addict's worst nightmare, to be stuck with a rock and no fire to light it. So I started walking around the house, knocking on doors. I hit three rooms without success, watching the faces jump into the light with fear in their eyes, knowing this was wrong but feeling that familiar itch up my arms and thinking, *It's only one hit. It's not a big deal. I can do one hit, or two, and go back to Club Surrender tomorrow and nobody will know. Nobody will ever know.*

Then I opened the fourth door and saw, right in the middle of the room, the heavy man from the shelter. He had a pipe in his hand, but otherwise he looked exactly like he did in front of the television. For a moment, we stared at each other, then he shook his head and bent down to take a blast. When I saw the flame reflected in his face, it was like the devil himself, shaking his head and saying, *I know you, Ted. I know exactly who you are.* And right then I knew I could never stand in front of that room again, never go back to Club Surrender, never put down the pipe that already felt like both a life preserver and an anchor in my hand.

CHAPTER 9

That first hit of crack had a physical effect, like an allergic reaction. My whole body started to tingle. I felt like I was busting out in hives, like I was poisoned, but it wasn't poison, it was . . . power, I guess, and I started to crave—physically crave in my muscles and bones—like I never had before. I had saved up a little money while sober, but I blew through it in days without even putting a dent in my craving, and I wanted more. I had that old feeling of crawling on my knuckles, pulling myself along with my fingernails like Jack the Ripper, searching for the next score.

I was practically living in crack houses: buildings, usually abandoned, where drug dealers both sold crack and provided a place to smoke it. A crack house is the raggedy end of drug addiction, the lowest of the low, but I didn't have a choice because I had no home but the shelter and nowhere else to smoke. The very first week, the house was raided by the cops. I was asleep on the floor, and they put a hand over my mouth, a gun in my back, and said, "Don't make a sound, a**hole." They lined us up against the wall—I almost pissed myself with relief when I saw they were cops and not executioners—and after they arrested the dealers, they told us,

"We're letting you go if you run, not walk, out of here, and never look back." I took off running and didn't stop for fifteen blocks. The crack house was across the street from Friends of the Homeless, and I knew if someone saw me I was out of SNP.

It wasn't long before I was out of SNP anyway. The routine that had sustained me felt like a straightjacket now, so I stopped participating in the counseling sessions, stopped cleaning the second-floor men's bunk area, never went back to Club Surrender. I moved into the general Friends of the Homeless population with the unrepentant crackheads, the lifers, and I slid right in with them, even visited their dope houses. I grew angry, bitter and angry. I wasn't smiling Ted Williams anymore. I was a man you didn't want to know. I was surly from dope sickness, sure, but mostly I was angry at myself, and I took that anger out on those around me.

One morning, I fell down the stairs. I wasn't even high. My left leg just gave out and I crashed, tumbling violently to the bottom without a chance to break my fall. As I lay in a hospital bed in terrible pain, I thought, *That's it, Ted. You're out of chances. God is through with you now.*

I was wrong. He never gives up. I know that now, but I couldn't see it then. I was in the devil's grip. The hospital gave me Vicodin and sent me back to Friends of the Homeless, and I ate my pills like candy, as many as I could stomach at a time. But Vicodin made me itch, so I took them out on the street, hunched and in pain, and traded them for crack. I still had my job at Kentucky Fried Chicken, so like an addict I started palming twenty-dollar bills, sticking them in my pocket instead of the cash register. I broke out in a sweat every time, too, not because I worried about stealing, but because every twenty-dollar bill was a rock, and I wanted that crack. I smoked after work, washed it down with the cheapest malt liquor, and came back to the homeless shelter later and later, surlier and surlier, until finally I got into a fight with a staffer and was kicked out.

So I found a woman and shacked up with her. Her name was Tara. I knew her from my old days as a disc jockey, a sweet girl once upon a time, now a crackhead down on Main Street, just like me. It was a destructive relationship. I was depressed, I was on a drug-smoking spree, and I didn't care what happened to anybody. I stole from KFC for our crack, and after I was fired, I got a job at another fast food restaurant and stole from them, too. I took my money and walked the street in the middle of the night, looking for a crack house. These were the worst blocks in Columbus at that time, the very bottom of street life, and I have a fair complexion, you know, thick straight hair. I looked like a white boy in a pot of black. Ducking down alleys with crackheads to take a blast, asking around for dope houses, that could have gotten me killed, but I didn't think twice. I went out, night after night, and it wasn't long before everybody knew my face, and then I was safe, because nobody was going to roll a desperate, ready-to-die junkie like me.

They didn't see Tara so much. I was the pickup man, the one who went out for drugs. She was the one waiting at the apartment, but half the time I didn't come home, and that drove her wild. She didn't care about me. We were both users, even sex was a hustle, a way to keep the roof over my head and the crack in her lungs. But she was paranoid behind the drugs. Aggressive. I was a good hustler, and she wanted to keep me, but she knew I was skipping out on her, and the longer we were together, the more we fought.

She finally lost it when I received some back pay, maybe a tax refund from my KFC job, I can't remember, and didn't come home for three days. She locked me out of the apartment and held my possessions hostage, demanding her share of the cash. It wasn't much, but she had some things I wanted, especially a scrapbook of my relationship with Lisa. So after a few days, I came up with the cash. She opened the door with a loving smile, but I didn't say a word. I just crammed my possessions into a pillowcase and ran.

I knew they wouldn't take me back at Friends of the Homeless, so I headed downtown to Faith Mission, where I experienced true homelessness for the first time. That's what I consider it anyway, because for me Friends of the Homeless was a self-betterment program. It was a temporary home. We slept sixty to a room, but I had an assigned bunk, guaranteed every night, and a secure place for my valuables. At Faith Mission, you checked out every morning at ten. You checked back in at five. If bunks were available, they'd give you a sheet and a pillow and tell you to find a spot. If the place was full, you were out of luck. In theory, the sheets and pillows were cleaned every day, but anybody could see that wasn't true. Half the time, there were no sheets at all.

There was no rehabilitation at Faith Mission. No counselors. The phone number of a help center was taped to the wall, but otherwise you were on your own. The staff's job was merely to break up fights, and their goal was to make sure everyone survived the night. There was no cleaning crew, no security guard. You kept your valuables with you at all times, even when you went to the bathroom, because if you turned your head for a second, your stuff was gone. And when I say valuables, I mean stuff valuable to you, because anything of true value—a camera, a watch—would be stolen right out of your hands, because the men in Faith Mission (and it was all men) weren't looking for a new life, they were just looking to get themselves high for another day.

Faith Mission was so bad I left after a few nights, but my next stop, Open Shelter, was even worse. Faith Mission at least had bunks, even if you had to scramble for one every night. Open Shelter (since demolished) was nothing but a warehouse for human beings, where residents slept on the floor in an unheated concrete room. If you were lucky, you arrived early enough for a pallet, but even then you'd be cursing your luck, because the pallets were stained and stank like hell. Half of them were crawling with bugs, but that was nothing compared to the bathrooms. The bathrooms at Open Shelter, like the pallets, were never cleaned. There was feces and vomit and mold in the toilet area, and the showers . . . let's just say no one ever took a shower at Open Shelter. I had enough wits left to find clean showers in old friends' houses or charity basements, but most people never showered at all.

The stink of those guys, though, that awful rotten odor, was nothing compared to their attitudes. Open Shelter was filled with nutcases and spiraling addicts, the kind who screamed at night. It was full of brain-damaged kids and schizophrenics with no one to care for them. I never talked to anybody there, because you never knew what you were going to get. Guys threw filth on your clean clothes or stepped on your new shoes out of simple hate. I saw drunks shivved and old men mugged out of spite, and every two weeks a crowd gathered outside the door, jockeying to be in prime position to steal the disability checks from the damaged. If you wanted to keep anything, even a photograph, you stuffed it in a bag and slept on it as your pillow. You slept on your shoes, too, or someone would steal them off your feet. That place was a cancer on society. There wasn't a single long-term resident in Open Shelter who was sane, because living like that drove you insane. And it drove many to drugs. There was an abandoned train trestle outside the place (also since demolished), and all night long you could see the

dealers moving up and down the row of huddled figures, and lighters flaring like fireflies and then dying out at the end of the line.

Jail didn't deter me. The loss of my family didn't stop me. But
the horror of Open Shelter? That got my attention. I beat it out of
there in a matter of days and talked my way into the most exclusive
shelter in town. The Salvation Army was less a shelter than a room-
ing house, where you received a shared room for three months in
exchange for labor. You had to be dedicated to recovery to be in
the Salvation Army, and I worked the recovery program like a desperate man. I talked to the counselors and went to daily devotion.
I watched videotapes of Father Martin, a formerly alcoholic Catholic priest who appealed to the white people, and black Brother Earl,
a former pimp with a blue-collar attitude. Those two put the love of
God back in my heart. With their help, I kept a steady routine, kept
busy, took a shower every day, ate right. I even got the first pick of
clothes from the donation ramp, where I worked for a few weeks,
and some of those clothes were stylish, too.

I also worked the kitchen, making meals for the other men in the
shelter. I had to wake up at five to start the prep, but I loved the
routine of those early mornings with my scrub brush and my paring
knife. That kitchen is where I met Eric, my first friend on the
streets.

Eric was young, probably mid-twenties, compared to my thirty-
five. He was a big guy, athletic, because he had been a football
player in high school. After graduation, some friends from the
team suggested they start dealing drugs. He wasn't going to college, his playing days were over, so he said, "Okay." He was from a
single-parent family, no siblings, and his mother was a drinker.
"Those guys became my family, you know, Ted. They took me in."

I knew. I'd had that same feeling. I'd never been a dealer, but I'd taken shortcuts to fit in. I'd cheated myself. By the time Eric's mother kicked him out of her house for lying around on the porch all day and refusing to get a legitimate job, he had a crack habit to match his dealing. Most of his high school friends were gone by then, dead or working or selling somewhere else, so he took to the streets. He became selfish in his addiction, he told me. He didn't think about anyone but himself and his needs, didn't worry about his friends, didn't call his mother for more than a year.

He stopped before he told me the next part, wiping away the sweat with his apron.

"When I finally called her, Ted, I could tell something was wrong. She said she wasn't feeling well, but I could tell it was more serious than that. So I kept pressing her, you know, until she finally admitted she'd had a stroke. Then she started crying. I thought she was going to hang up, but instead she said, 'You're killing me, Eric. I worry about you every day, son, and it's killing me.'"

He checked himself into the Salvation Army the next day. He was sixty days clean when I met him, and he was calling his mother three times a day. When he got out, he said, he was going home to Dayton to see her.

It wasn't too many days later that I called my momma for the first time since Friends of the Homeless. My father answered. "Are you working?"

"No, sir," I said.

He handed the phone to my momma without another word.

"Teddy?" I could hear the relief in her voice.

"Momma. Oh, Momma."

"Are you working, Teddy?"

"I'm working at the Salvation Army, Momma. I'm in a program to get clean."

There was silence on the line, and I could tell she didn't know what to think. She had hope, I guess, but even then, after four years of crack addiction and arrests, she didn't have faith. She didn't believe in me, and I was desperate for her belief.

"I don't have a home, Momma. I don't have nothing anymore."

"You have a home, Teddy. You will always have a home right here. But you got to leave that life behind."

I started crying like a baby, like that little boy that ran to his momma every time his father tanned his hide. "I'm trying, Momma. I'm trying. I promise you, I'm trying real hard."

CHAPTER 10

I spent three months at the Salvation Army. I completed their program, and it might have been the first program I ever completed in my life. I felt good about that, really good. I felt like I was going to make it, because I was talking with my momma, I was going to church, I got baptized, I truly had God in my heart for the first time in twenty years. Not my momma's God, not my daddy's God, but *my* God this time, the one that spoke directly to me. That's what the Salvation Army was about: not a physical treatment but a spiritual cleanse. A new way of thinking. I had lived so long for me, me, me, but when I thought about God, I thought about something outside of myself. I realized I was part of a bigger world, and that doing right wasn't just important, it was the only way to a meaningful life.

I remember especially Proverbs 5–6: *Acknowledge Him in all your ways.* That verse really touched me. It became my focus, every day, to acknowledge Him. It helped me identify and make the good choices, but it also reminded me of the world beyond my own needs. Acknowledging God made me think of other people, and that's invaluable to an addict because addiction is deeply selfish, and my lifelong struggle with selfishness had led me down the path of ruin. I had love in my heart for everyone in those days. I had a smile on my face all the time, because I'd embraced so many positive teachings. *Give it up to God. Don't be hungry, angry, lonely, or tired. Progress, not perfection.*

I was on the circuit, as we called it, staying away from crack houses by walking to different corners three to five times a day to receive charity meals and snacks. The church people in the vans didn't remember me, but some of the longtimers knew me from the old days, when Lisa and I walked the circuit with our kids. The circuit was a community, a subset of the homeless population that got together for a few hours a day, then went its separate ways. A lot of the guys weren't strictly homeless. They rented a room in one of the downtown tenements and walked the circuit for meals. Most had some form of disability, physical or mental, a lot had phobias, but quite a few were sharp. They'd call out, "Hey, Radio, where you been?"

Everyone on the street knew me as Radio. It was a description, sure, because I'd been a radio man, but it was also a term of respect. I had talent, and everyone on the street recognized it. When I wasn't spiraling on crack, I was a people person. I'd slap the dirtiest man on the back, shake his hand, treat him like a friend, tell him, "You're riding with Ted Williams, brother, nothing but the hottest jams, right here on the corner of Second and Grand."

I'd be on line at the soup kitchen, and I'd hear someone say, "That's him. That's the guy with the radio voice."

"Hey, man," his friend would say. "Let me hear it."

I'd smile. "Don't forget, tomorrow morning at ten is your chance to win."

"Oh, yeah," they'd say. "I heard you, man."

I'd give them "Southeast Seafood, for the freshest clams" or "USA Pawn, dusk until dawn," or one of my other commercials, since some stations were still playing ads I cut years before.

Or I'd make up a lie. "You hear that new promo: *Don't miss Family Guy, weeknights at eleven on WABE?*"

"Yeah, I heard it. That's you?"

"Sure is."

"Well, good for you, Radio. Good for you." We'd move a little further up the line, waiting for our half-sandwich or a cup of soup. "Say, you still seeing that fine woman you used to come around with? What was her name?"

"Lisa? No, I'm not seeing her right now."

"Oh, I'm sorry. She take those kids with her? They adorable kids."

I didn't tell them I had a new woman, Theresa, who I met at Friends of the Homeless. Or that I had a new baby, a gorgeous girl, I hadn't known about until Theresa tracked me down at the Salvation Army. We were living together because I thought that's what God wanted, but it wasn't working because I still had my heart set on Lisa. My primary reason for getting sober, in fact, was to get Lisa back. I was obsessed with that goal, because I never stopped loving her. Even though I hadn't seen her in a year, I thought about her all the time. Not Patty and my children, my real responsibilities, but Lisa. If I could get clean, I thought, and get an apartment, and prove I was a man, she'd take me back, and we'd have our family again.

So Theresa and I split, and I went to the VA hospital in Chillicothe, Ohio, for their twenty-eight day detox, because, unfortunately, for all my best intentions, I was still smoking a little crack. I'd tell myself it was all right, that if I kept my attitude positive and

God's love in my prayers, I'd keep my worst days behind me. But an addiction is never behind you, especially if you indulge it. I can't remember if I lasted the whole twenty-eight-day detox that first time, because between 1994 and 1996, I did four stints in rehab at Chillicothe. I completed it once. The other times, I'd last a week, maybe two weeks, and I'd feel so great about myself that I'd go right back to Columbus and score a hit.

It was addiction, sure, but it wasn't the spiraling kind I'd been in with Lisa, where nothing matters but the drug, where you lose your morals, your common sense, your kids . . . everything. There are phases of addiction, even within one addict's life, and for a time I was able to use but not lose. I still had my perspective. I had goals. The need to feed my addiction didn't destroy what I'd achieved in recovery, but it kept me from moving forward, held me in a spot just below the ability to rent an apartment and move back into the normal world. I'd get a job at McDonald's or Burger King, save a little money, then start spending a few evenings down on Champion and Main scoring hits, maybe ducking into the alley with some brothers from the soup line. I'd been drifting for more than four years by this time and I was a well-liked figure in the homeless community. Everybody knew Ted Williams was a hugger, a giver, earned his keep, didn't have any violence in him. So I'd duck up into an acquaintance's house for a few days, or stay with my buddy Eric from the Salvation Army. He'd relapsed like me, but he'd gone back to the Salvation Army while I was in Chillicothe and cleaned up for good. He had a job in maintenance at a city building and was making money, so he'd take me in for a while and we'd attend Narcotics Anonymous meetings together.

I met my second friend on the street, Al Battle, at those NA meetings. Al was a recovering addict, but he wasn't homeless. He was a musician, had a band with an old friend he'd rescued from the street, but he made most of his money promoting concerts. He heard my voice—"I'm Ted Williams, and I'm a drug addict"—and knew immediately I had talent. So he introduced himself. He started driving me to meetings, and then we'd often drink coffee together. After a few months of friendship, Al started throwing me voice work in commercials promoting his concerts on the radio. That was a proud moment, when I heard my voice in a new ad on the radio. That gave me hope. It made me realize I was still "Ted Williams, the Golden Voice," and that made me believe I was going to make it back.

But I never made it. Instead, every time I found a little success, I'd fall heavier into crack. Then my fingers would wander into the cash register at Wendy's or wherever I was working at the time, and I'd go on a little bender. Eric would kick me out because my crack smoking endangered his own recovery, and I'd end up at Faith Mission or on the street. Eventually, I'd check myself back into the Salvation Army and start the process over again, a little better, a little more clean, every time.

The Relapse King, that's what they called me. "Why don't Radio make it?" some new guy would ask an old-timer. "The man has talent."

"Who, Radio? He's the Relapse King."

It wasn't a bad life, not compared to what I'd lived. No responsibilities. No crushing needs. Nobody to hurt. Not much crime. I'd have drifted with it, I suppose, maybe eventually gotten myself a tenement like those soup kitchen regulars, a habit I could handle, if I didn't still dream. Those calls of, "Radio, how you been?"; those lies I told about being on the air; those brothers and sisters who said, "You're not one of us, you can be somebody"—they were like needles to my soul.

I didn't have contacts. I didn't have a reputation anyone would trust. But I had my voice, and when I went to the edge and found myself once again in some rat-infested hole, ankle deep in the chore of a dozen pipes, it was my voice that carried me out.

God wouldn't give me this gift and let me waste it, I told myself, lighting another stem. *God's going to give me another chance.*

I think it was one of the brothers in the food line who told me about a new oldies station, 107.5 FM. "They been saying it on the air, Radio. They looking for a disc jockey."

I was fresh out of my last stint at the VA in Chillicothe. I'd been clean for a few months, so there was no reason not to try. They weren't going to take me back at WCKX, but a new station might take a chance on an oldie-but-goodie, broken-down-but-top-of-the-line. I took a shower at a buddy's place, put on my best pair of Salvation Army threads, and took the bus to the station. I walked in the door and saw a familiar-looking man standing in the lobby. He looked at me for a minute, like he was sizing me up, then pointed his finger and said, "John Wayne."

"No, sir. I'm Ted Williams."

"That's right, Ted Williams. I knew it was somebody famous." He turned to the gentleman beside him, a young cat a decade or more behind me, and said, "Hire this man."

I could see it in the youngblood's eyes: *Hell no.* But before he could say it, I grabbed the first man's hand and said, "Thank you, sir. Thank you. I won't let you down."

Then I closed my eyes and said, *Thank you, Jesus. Thank you for my second chance.*

CHAPTER 11

The man in the lobby's name was Horace Perkins, and it turned out he owned the station. He had been a high-powered production manager back in the day, but he was out of the game for a while and finally decided to buy his way back in. He's dead now, God rest his soul, but there haven't been many people in my life better than Horace Perkins. Radio's a dirty business, top to bottom, but that man was straight. Never cut a corner to make a dollar at someone else's expense, always had his hand out to help his fellow man. He knew my history, or at least knew my behavior at the top and the rumors of my fall, but he had a giving heart. He knew I was homeless, so the first day I worked there, he cosigned a lease to get me an apartment a few blocks from the station. He even advanced my first check so I could pay for it. I could have run off to the crack house without working a day—there were times, whole years, when I was sick enough to have done just that—but Mr. Perkins's trust made me a better man. He knew talent, and he trusted me, no questions asked.

With his production manager, the young cat from the lobby, it was different. The production manager was the boss of the broadcast. He hired the talent—which was why he always had problems with me, since I was forced on him—scheduled the disc jockeys, and made sure the on-air operation ran smooth. He didn't make budgets or sell ads, but he made sure the ads got played. There was no way that cat was putting me on the air, not with his job on the line, so he stuck me in the production booth.

It took me ten minutes to realize radio wasn't like it used to be. Back in my day, disc jockeys were free rovers. We were personalities. We made decisions about what to play and said whatever we wanted on the air. There were rules—certain songs had to be played, certain words couldn't be said, the station had to be identified on-air—but all the energy came out of the booth. When I opened a mike, I was playing off the sound of my last record, and when I closed the mike I was leading into the next song's jump. If I did a good job of that day after day, I could make a difference to the station. Sometimes, in those days, the disc jockey was the bottom line.

At WJZA, most of the music came from a subscription service, so we played the same songs, in mostly the same order, that a bunch of similar stations were playing in other markets. Instead of a board full of buttons to crash through every fifteen minutes, and actual records to drop onto turntables, there were tape reels that played twenty or thirty minutes at a stretch. The disc jockey simply opened the mike when the reel ended, and when he closed the mike he simply hit the button for the next reel. The music distributor was choosing the singles and making the hits, not the disc jockey, and maybe that's how it should be, I don't know, but I still missed Hank Spann and Murray the K.

I'm not saying I didn't like WJZA, *107.5, playing a better mix of yesterday's hits and today's jams.* It was a good station run the right way. I was happy to be working in the back, even if the production booth was miles away from the actual station in an industrial area of town and, because of the late hours, I often missed the last bus home. I wasn't on the air, I wasn't near the air, but I was in radio again, even if my job was mostly splicing local commercials onto the reels. It wasn't much, but I loved it because it was radio, man, *radio*—and it was better than Burger King.

Pretty soon, I started recording commercials. This was safe work for the station since commercials were recorded in a sound studio, not live. If I messed up, we just taped again. It was good for the clients, too, because they got Ted Williams's voice at a below-market price, and there wasn't anything like it. My voice was still exactly as it had been in the old days, and if I had to work harder on my delivery than I used to—no one-takes this time around—the final product still rang out and attracted attention. A lot of my old clients came back, and a lot of new clients signed up, too, including my friend Al Battle, the concert promoter who'd given me work when I was on the street.

After a few months, Horace Perkins offered me the midday shift. It was low profile, but it was seven years since I'd been on the air, almost ten since I'd been number one in Columbus, and I was thankful for the opportunity. Besides, what I did, the big voice, wasn't in style anymore. Understatement was the calling card, sincerity and control. The goal wasn't to sound like you were reaching a million people at once, but speaking to each listener individually, especially since WJZA was an easy-listening station. I'd been listening to the broadcasts in the booth long enough to understand the sound, and I'd been practicing at home, so I was ready to be the new Ted Williams, the smooth lover not the wild man. Between my commercials and my air shifts, it wasn't long before WJZA was making good money off my golden voice.

My benefits? They were even greater. I had a regular routine. I
had my voice on the radio. I had my own apartment. I didn't have
anything in it but a bed and a pot, but I was cooking my own food,
cleaning my own space, brushing my teeth over a sink. I was clean.
I was talking to my momma again, and occasionally my dad. I even
started talking with Patty on the telephone a couple times a week,
trying to win back her trust.

It was the children who brought us together. Julia and Jenay, my
two youngest daughters (thirteen and eleven at that time) heard me
on the radio, and they wanted me back in their lives. They were so
hungry for their father, they begged Patty to call me, even after the
abandonment, the broken promises, the day spent smoking crack in
the park while little Jenay cried. Patty eventually agreed, so over a few
months I eased my way back into their lives: picked the children up
for "dates" to the ice cream store or took them on a tour of the radio
station. It made me so proud for my children to see their daddy working, to take them to my office and introduce them around. It made
them proud, too, because Daddy wasn't only back in their lives, he
didn't just have a job, he had a *cool* job—he played music and met
famous people. The money was tight since I was making three hundred a week and paying four hundred dollars a month in rent, but
with my children's love and my recovery mantras, I could manage.

One day at a time. One step at a time. Be grateful for what you got.

The ultimate goal, though, was still Lisa, lovely Lisa. I was putting my life together for her. I was happy to spend time with my
children, I was happy to be a father again, but it was Lisa I dreamed
about. Not Patty. Not my parents. And certainly not God. I had
Him in my prayers, but I didn't have Him in the center of my life.
I was asking, asking, but what was I giving back? I was still building
a house of sand.

Then WJZA scheduled an old-school concert to celebrate its first year on the air, and I saw my chance. The lineup featured the Ohio Players, Roger Troutman, and Con Funk Shun. I knew Lisa loved Michael Cooper of Con Funk Shun; she'd always wanted to meet him. It was the perfect opportunity to comp her a backstage pass and show her I was back in the game.

We'd seen each other only once since we split. About six months later, I dropped by her apartment unannounced, with a rock in my pocket, and ruined her sobriety. Again. That was three years before, but Lisa was still angry. When I called her about the concert, that's what she talked about, losing her sobriety because of me, and losing our kids.

But I didn't hear it. I didn't notice that she talked like my momma, with happiness for my progress but without belief. All I heard was that she was coming to the concert.

And then I saw her. She was sitting across the lobby at the concert hall, alone on a bench. She had red lips and light skin and a nice tight dress, just like the old days, and those dresses always lit up a room. Time had aged her, sure, but she looked fresh, like she'd never smoked crack in her life. It was like she came walking straight out of my dreams into my reality, lovely Lisa, the answer to all my prayers.

I went up and gave her a hug. (She felt good.)

I told her I was six months sober. (She was happy for me.)

I told her I was working in radio again. (She knew.)

I told her I missed her, that I'd found God, that I was finally man enough to take care of her and be a father to our boys . . .

And then her man walked up. It was Kip, her ex-boyfriend, the one who'd been in prison when Lisa and I first met. The way he put his arm around her, and the way she grabbed him around the waist in return, told me everything I needed to know. They were to-gether, and they wanted me to know it.

She didn't hate me. That was obvious. But what she felt was worse. She felt nothing. All those years I'd been dreaming about her, and Lisa hadn't been thinking about me at all.

So I turned and walked away. Went backstage. It was like old times. I was being greeted by name—"Ted Williams from the radio, how you doing, man, come meet somebody"—by people I didn't know. I was introduced to producers and managers. I was with the band. But it wasn't the same, not without Lisa. I saw old friends, other people I'd invited to the show, but it wasn't the same. They came up to me—"Great show!"—but I just nodded and shook their hands.

"Thanks for the passes, man."

"Nah, it's no big deal."

I was standing at the side of the stage, alone in the crowd, when I felt a hand on my back. An old friend had a new girl, and she was impressed by his backstage passes.

"Thank you!" he yelled over the noise. "You're my boy!" Then he leaned close and said, "Something for you," and slipped that some-thing into my hand.

Round, rough, smaller than a golf ball. I knew immediately what it was, although we didn't call it a golf ball since no ghetto black ever played that game. We called it an eight ball, because it was an eighth of a gram of rock cocaine, and every user has heard of pool.

I should have thrown it out. I should have tossed it on the floor and walked away. But I couldn't. I hated that rock. I couldn't look at it, but I couldn't let it go. I kept it clutched in my hand for the rest of the show, telling myself, *Just one smoke.* Then, *No, throw it away.* Then, *Hold on to it. Sell it. That rock is worth a hundred at least.*

But I'd never sold crack in my life. Who was I going to sell it to? But holding on to it, hour after hour, made my heart sick. I felt like I was eating my own stomach. But losing Lisa made me feel worse. And the whole time I argued with myself about what to do, another thought was swirling in my head: *What else you got, Ted? What else you got to lose?*

Around three in the morning, I walked into a mean-looking convenience store near my apartment. I didn't look at anybody, kept my eyes on the floor.

"Rose," I said to the counterman.

He put a glass tube on the counter. It was round, thicker than a pen when you take the ink cartridge out, but only half as long. Inside was a tiny rose. That's why users call it a stem, because of that little sacrificial rose.

"Scrub," I said.

He took a Brillo pad and placed it in a bag without a word.

"Lighter."

I slid a few dollars across the counter and left without looking back. Fifteen minutes later, I was in my apartment, my hand trembling as I tore a piece off the Brillo pad and shoved it into the stem. I felt tears on my cheeks as I broke a thumbtack-size piece off the rock and jammed it into the tip. I struck the lighter. I held the flame to the rock, and I was bawling like Pookie in *New Jack City* when the crack started to glow.

CHAPTER 12

Within a week it was over. I lasted exactly two more shifts on the air. I had blown through my money by then, without any ability or willingness to stop. I was an hour into my second shift when a local promoter called me in the booth. The comedian Tommy Davidson was in town for a show that night, and advance ticket sales were slow. "If I bring Tommy by in fifteen minutes, will you put him on the air?"

"For two hundred dollars."

"Done."

I opened the mike for Tommy, and one minute into the interview the red button on my console started to blink. I ignored it, because I knew who it was. It was the production manager, wondering what was going on. Five seconds after Tommy and the promoter left, he was in the booth.

"What was that, Ted?"

"Just giving a brother a break."

He knew what was up. Pay for play. He fired me on the spot. Soon after, I lost my apartment. Didn't matter, I wasn't going home much anyway. I was on Champion and Main, or over on Bryden

Road, or anywhere else the dope was hot. I was in another period of self-destruction, but worse than ever this time. I'd blown it, and I knew it, so I was empty: no hopes, no dreams, no self-respect. Nothing mattered. Nothing but crack, because when you fall off the wagon, especially after six months of sobriety, you fall hard. There's so much self-hatred, so much disappointment, that you disappear straight into your addiction.

I stopped calling Momma. I stopped calling my kids. I was supposed to take Patty to dinner and a jazz show the week after the concert. It was Father's Day, and we were going to talk about reconciling. There was a real chance, with Lisa out of the picture, that we were going to get back together and raise our kids. Instead, while Patty sat waiting for me, I was in a crack house, blowing off the top of my head. She called me only once after that, to tell me how devastated the children were, how high their hopes had been, and how bitterly I'd let them down.

By then, I was too far gone. I was smoking crack every day, camping out in the storage closet at my friend Master Nick Ray's karate studio, a place I often turned to in times of trouble. I was sitting there on a dirty blanket a few weeks later, grieving for my lost chances, smoking myself senseless, when I got a call from an old friend, a successful businessman I'd known since my first days in radio.

"Hey, Ted. Listen, man. I'm downtown and I need you to come rescue me. Take a taxi. I've got money."

He gave me an address. Ten minutes later, I was on the eighth floor of a nasty ghetto tenement, knocking on a metal door. It opened. A woman was on the other side, staring at me. She was clean and well scrubbed, with meat on her bones and a great figure, but she was a junkie. She had that look in her eyes, that hard hunger, and I thought, *What's going on here? Who is this white bitch?*

It was Kathy Chambers, the woman who changed my life. Up until that moment my street life had been all about Ted Williams. I didn't know it at the time, but from then on, it was Kathy and Ted.

Kathy

When I was two years old, my mother developed multiple sclerosis. The doctors told her not to have any more kids, but ten months later she had my younger sister, her fifth child. She never recovered, and I don't have any memories of her not in a wheelchair, paralyzed from the waist down. My father was an alcoholic. He couldn't take care of her, so he put her in a nursing home. My two older sisters had a different father, so they left the family, and my dad's mother stepped in to take care of us. She died a few months later, and we moved to Kings Mills, Ohio, a small community outside Cincinnati. My father brought us to Columbus once a month to see my mother in the nursing home, but he'd never go in. I don't know what he did. Drink, I guess. I'd sit on my mother's lap and talk to her, but she couldn't talk back. She sat in her wheelchair and barely moved, but she watched me with her eyes. I could see how much she loved me in those eyes, even when I cried.

My father had a live-in girlfriend, and she was nothing like my mom, or what I thought my mom was like. My stepmom was an alcoholic, and my father used to beat her. He cracked her head. He broke her arm. She always had black eyes. To me, she was worse than him, though, just a real bad drunk. My father never would have hurt me, not physically anyway, but my stepmom was dangerous. She didn't care about me, and I truly believed, at five years old, that she was capable of killing me and my kid sister. My brother, who was two years older than me, kept us safe. He was my best friend and protector.

Whenever we became too much, or the drinking became too much, the three of us went to Children's Services. It was for our own safety, but I didn't know that at the time. My mother had five brothers, and they wanted to take care of us, but my father wouldn't hear it. He hated my mother's family. So we stayed in foster homes. Then we'd come home, and someone would get their arm broken, and we'd be back with strangers for a while. Every few weeks I'd sit with my mother in the nursing home, but I didn't tell her much about my life. I always tried not to cry, because I didn't want to hurt her, and I didn't want to ruin the best day of the month. So when I found out my uncle adopted a little girl who was only a week older than me, I just hugged my mom, or what was left of her, and wouldn't let go.

Finally, my dad put us in a children's home in Cincinnati. I was seven; my sister Christine was five; my brother David, nine. We stuck together for a while, tried to keep our heads down, but it wasn't long before David was getting into trouble, smoking cigarettes and skipping classes, talking back. I came right along with him, following his lead. We ran away when I was twelve, and by then I was smoking weed. We lived under bridges and scrounged for food and fell in with some hard drug addicts, real bad guys with no business being around little kids. It was friendly at first. They gave us a place to sleep. It was an abandoned building, but it was all right. Then one of them took me into a back room. I remember burnt spoons and broken needles. Smashed glass. A filthy corner of the floor. And screaming, lots of screaming. But the more I screamed the more he enjoyed it and the worse it got. It was violent rape. Extremely violent. And bloody. Very bloody. He wanted to hurt me. And he did.

The police caught us the next day and brought us back to the home, but I went wild. Self-destructive wild. I felt like I was born bad, born into sin, and there was nothing good inside me, and nothing good would ever happen to me. I'd felt that way since I was a little girl, and my life was nothing but proof. I don't ever remember being happy as a kid, not even on my mother's lap. How can you be happy when your mother's sick and she's dying a little more every time you see her, and she's the only person in the world who loves you?

The children's home shipped me back to my dad's house in Kings Mills with my brother, because he was worse than me. My father was busy drinking himself to death, and my stepmom was doing the same, so there was nothing in the house but booze. No food. No bedtimes. There was no supervision on the best of days, and even less after my dad and stepmom went to visit her kids in Tennessee. While down there, they got into a serious car accident and my father almost died. After a couple weeks, when he still wasn't out of the hospital, my brother and I realized nobody was coming back. I was fifteen. He was seventeen. We drank and smoked weed, stayed up late, skipped school. It wasn't fun because I didn't like drugs. I didn't like having older boys around. I didn't like not being in control of my body. I had read *Go Ask Alice*, about a girl driven to prostitution by drugs, and it scared me to death. But what else did I know?

After a month, someone called Children's Services. Even our

white-trash neighbors knew that what was happening in our house wasn't right, especially after my thirteen-year-old sister joined us. We were five minutes from being wards of the state when my older half-sisters, Colleen and Darla, who had grown up with their own father and hadn't been in our lives since I was five, arrived. They took us to Columbus, and Darla put us up in her small two-bedroom apartment. She fed us. She bought us clothes. She even sent us to Catholic school. She was seven years older than me, so I thought she was an adult. But she was only twenty-two. She was newly married, just starting as a hairdresser. She didn't have money for clothes, much less Catholic school. But she paid on an installment plan, because she thought those schools could save us.

They didn't. That summer I stole from my sister Colleen's store (first time, but definitely not the last) and ran away to Florida with my younger sister. That's where everyone went who wanted a new start, to Florida, with the sun. It took one day before we were conned out of everything we owned, and by the end of the summer I was back in Columbus. The Catholic school wouldn't have me, so Darla sent me to a reform school for troubled girls. Somehow, I made it to the eleventh grade before I dropped out and enrolled in beauty school. I wasn't qualified because the school required a high school diploma, but Darla got me in. I went for a few months before meeting the man of my dreams. He was just a kid like me, but he was the son of a preacher, he was studying for the ministry, and I knew if a man like that could love me, I wasn't all bad. He brought my spirit back. He gave me hope. I turned seventeen on February 13, 1978, and we were married two weeks later. Two years later, he was slammed head-on by a drunk driver on his way to a Sunday morning church service. The steering wheel lacerated his heart and he died instantly. It might as well have lacerated my heart, too, because that accident tore everything out of me that he had ever put in.

I went back to beauty school, but I fell into depression and the bottle. Then my mother died. I cannot tell you how painful that was for me. Ever since I was a little girl, I lived with the fantasy that one day my mother would rise out of her wheelchair, walk out of that convalescent home, and take me back. I saw it every night when I went to bed. I wished for it every day when my stepmom raised her fist. I didn't pray for it, because I was cursed and I had no right to pray, but I held it in my heart. It was a child's dream, of course, even if I was no longer a child. My mother had been paralyzed for years. She was broken, and death was the best thing for her. I knew that. But I still dreamed. When she died, all my dreams died, too.

A few weeks after her death, I met my second husband. I don't know why he fell for me. I don't know why any man ever fell for me. In my mind, I was overweight. I was ugly. I was a dead-end, born loser and a child of sin. I think maybe men saw that, and they wanted to save me. That's all I can see, that maybe they were on the other side of the same window looking in while I was looking out, because I was desperate to be saved. Why else would a good Christian man, with eight years of college and a new car, bother with a woman like me?

He took me out of my sister's house. He set me up in my own apartment. Eventually, we fell in love and he moved in. He was an over-the-road trucker, and for three years we drove tandem. At first, I loved it. It was exciting. We saw forty-eight states. But eventually the lifestyle started to wear on me. I grew tired of the road. I wanted to be home. We hit a bad stretch on a cross-country trip, where we both had a serious case of food poisoning. We were on the road between Phoenix and Los Angeles, which is a bald desert a hundred miles from anywhere. I spilled a carton of milk, it was 120 degrees, and I was sick from both ends. I said, "That's it. I've had enough."

I'm ashamed of what happened next. I really am. My husband was a good man. He bought me a house. He gave me a home. He made me his wife, and he loved me. He accepted me for who I was, and he changed me for the better. Even today, I've kept his last name. I don't deserve it. I shouldn't be in his life in any way. But that name was the only good part of me.

I can't blame what happened on my upbringing. I have three sisters and they all own businesses. They all married good men. My younger sister started the wrong way, like me, but when she turned her life around, she stayed that way. Not me. I got my chance, but I threw it away. Took my happy home and gambled it, first on poker, then on the horses. It was a family tradition. My father hosted all-night poker games. My brother bet on everything. Even my grandmother stayed up for days playing poker with her old-lady friends.

My habit started small, poker with my brother and his friends. That was how our relationship worked. I followed my brother. He was my inspiration, I guess, but also my best friend. I idolized him. He introduced me to alcohol, weed, strength in the face of adversity, kind words, and almost every man I ever dated, including my two husbands.

Gambling started as a social activity because I was lonely while my husband was on the road. It wasn't long, though, before I was hooked. I was hitting two horse tracks a day and taking advances against my checking account. I was overdrawn a thousand dollars a few times, but my father bailed me out (he survived the car accident but never stopped drinking), or my husband's next paycheck covered it, until one day it didn't. By then, I was deeply in debt to a man I'd met playing cards. He was thirty years older than me, married with five kids, but he was a serious alcoholic and hadn't really been with his wife in fifteen years. One day, he started handing me money and chips at the poker table, and pretty soon he was buying me perfume, tennis bracelets, and brand-name shoes. Finally, he said, "How do you think you're going to pay me back?"

The figure he mentioned was ten thousand dollars. I believed him. I said, "Um, do you want me to do something to make it even?"

"No," he said, and slipped me a thousand dollars to play the horses. I think I fell in love right then. Not with him, so much, but the money. I've always been partial to money. I didn't count sheep when I was young, I counted dollar bills, because money was going to take me away from it all. That's how I thought. No matter what the problem—loneliness, rape, abuse, my own deceit— money would make it right. I'd take my mother away from her wheelchair. I'd take my little sister away from the children's home. I had a sickness for money as bad as my sickness for men. I thought they both were the answer.

So I took the gifts: furniture, watches, bowling balls and fishing poles for my husband. My sugar daddy became good friends with my husband, and after that the money kept coming. He was a terrible alcoholic, drank Crown Royal all day and all night, and grifters loved to see him walking in the door because he was a soft touch, and he always had money. He kept it in a big black leather pouch around his waist, and it never seemed to run out.

One night, he passed out on my couch, and I looked into his pouch. It was jammed full of hundred-dollar bills. I think it was his retirement. He'd taken it in cash. So I took a few bills and shoved them under my mattress. He never noticed. So the next time he passed out, I took another fistful of bills.

Eventually, I told my husband I was moving out. I bought a condo in a nice part of Columbus, across the hall from my brother, and I had $35,000 in the bank that I'd lifted from the old man. My husband stuck with me. That's the kind of man he was. He was a good Christian, full of love, strength, and hope. He knew I had a gambling problem, but he believed in me. He believed I was a good person. He stayed until he came to my condo one afternoon and heard a man in my bedroom. I tried to apologize, but it was no use. He knew then I couldn't be saved.

Why did I do it? I don't know. I didn't believe in my own salvation, I guess. I thought I had bad blood and an evil destiny and nothing could be done about it. But it wasn't my blood. I chose that life. Gambling. Drinking. I even had a third man on the side, a friend of my brother. He was like me, a gambler and an addict, but I thought I loved him. Until my husband walked away. The minute that door closed, I fell into depression. We were married ten years. He was my good life. He tried to teach me patience and kindness, but I never learned. The day his letter arrived, apologizing but insisting on divorce, I was more hopeless than I'd ever been. I was as broken as the day my mother died, because this was on me. It was my fault. I sat on my bed and asked myself if I wanted to live or die. I didn't have an answer.

So I went across the hall and asked my brother for a hit.

My brother and his girlfriend had been smoking crack for years. He was my best friend and I was close to his girlfriend, but I was terrified of what that drug had done to them: paranoia, poverty, fear of the phone. He didn't want to give me that life, and I didn't want to take it but it felt inevitable, so I kept asking. I needed medicine for my pain. I needed something to take away my dark cloud.

Crack took it away. That first hit . . . euphoria. No world. No pain. Just the best feeling of my life. I can't describe it, except to say there was pleasure in every way. Body. Mind. Soul. That's why we do it, of course. Because of that one hit that rings our bell. Ten minutes in heaven. You never get back there, not like the first time, but you spend a lifetime chasing it.

And I chased it, all the way out of my sugar-daddy relationship, through my savings, and into a job at White Castle. Then Burger King. Then God knows where. I took a job at Speedway, grabbed three hundred dollars out of the cash register on the first day—after letting my brother and boyfriend rob the place—and never went back. I kept my car but I lost my condo, so I moved in with my brother. He was a genius at phone sales, always had been, but he'd been out of legitimate work for years. He taught me to work a hustle and I bilked a thousand dollars in two weeks, mostly out of our friends and relatives. Then I got high, crashed my car, and broke most of the bones in my body. I didn't quit. I used the insurance money for more: more gambling, more crack. I ran through my brother's lousy friends, each worse than the last. It wasn't until I met Carl, another friend of my brother, that I saw a way out.

Carl was messed up, too, but he was moving to a small town a couple hundred miles away. He was getting out. So I asked him to take me along. I didn't love him. Didn't even care for him that much. But I couldn't quit alone. I thought I needed a man. I always have.

So I moved to a small town with my new boyfriend. Hung out

with his nice Christian family, got a job in a sit-down restaurant, and stayed clean for a few years. Eventually, Carl started to get physically abusive, and I started to look for another man to save me. I left Carl for the cowboy who punched him out in a bar one night when he started to slap me around. I moved to West Virginia with the cowboy and got a good job as a hairdresser. I stayed off crack. But I drank. And I smoked. I crashed another car, broke my sternum in two. So my life was starting to unravel, even before my sister Colleen called.

"Your brother has bone cancer."

"How bad?"

"They give him a year."

By the time I got to Columbus, Davey had lost fifty pounds. He was in a wheelchair. His face was sunk, his skull stuck out, and he didn't look like himself. He looked like our mother. He motioned me over and whispered, "Hatty," because that was his special name for me. "Hatty, let's smoke a little bit."

This was my best friend, ever since I was a girl. Two years before, he seemed healthy. Now he looked like a corpse. I could see every bone in his hand when he reached for me, and the cartilage in between. His lips were white. They were coming right off his face. He was only thirty-seven, and he barely had the strength to lick them.

I told him, "No, Davey, I can't do that. I'm through."

He didn't mean anything. We had fun on that drug and now it was the only peace he was ever going to have. It was his only happiness, and he wanted to share it with his best friend. But I said no.

Then one day, I came over and Sharon, his girlfriend, was lifting him out of his wheelchair. He was nothing but bones. A skull on skin. He couldn't even hold his head up. He could barely moan. I watched him settle into bed and slowly, painfully, put the pipe to his lips, and I said, "I'll take a hit with you, Davey."

I took the pipe. I looked into his tired eyes. I took a hit. He smiled, sort of, and I went straight to the bottom. It was like drowning. I couldn't breathe, but I couldn't come up for air either. All I could do was hit the pipe.

Davey was given an apartment through social security since he was terminal. It was in a tenement in High Rise, one of the worst parts of Columbus. He never moved in. He went into hospice instead. So Sharon and I moved in, and we buried our sorrow in crack.

My sisters called every day. They pleaded, "Please come, Kathy, Davey's dying," but I couldn't. I couldn't face it. I couldn't sleep, couldn't eat, all I could do was chase, chase, chase, but there was nothing on the other end of the pipe. Nothing but death.

I finally went to see him. As soon as he looked at me, I started crying. He whispered, "Don't cry, Hatty, be strong," but I couldn't stop. All I could do was cradle his head in my lap, feel the skin on top of his cancerous bones.

He closed his eyes and muttered, "Don't cry at my funeral. Put a joint in my casket. Have a good time."

But how was I going to have a good time? I was drowning. How was I going to live, after my only friend died in my arms?

I don't remember the funeral. I just remember chasing, chasing, chasing, running up Sharon's credit card, overdrawing her bank account. Our relatives gave a thousand dollars to help Sharon through without David, and we blew it on crack. We didn't have furniture. We didn't have jobs. We were two white women in a pitch-black, crime-ridden part of Columbus, strung out on heartbreak and despair. We smoked for two weeks before running out of money and agreeing to clean my cousin's apartment for three hundred dollars. A crack dealer from the building drove us there. At a gas station on the way back, I noticed a good-looking black man with a nice suit and a new car. I gave him my phone number. Two days later, he was in our tenement apartment with a fistful of crack, and Sharon and I plunged into another binge. After three days without sleep, we didn't have the energy to leave, not even for rock, but the man said, "I know someone."

Two hits later, I opened the door to a skinny man with a big smile. I took one look and thought, *Who is this guy?* The color of his skin. The texture of his hair. He was exotic. He looked white, but he was obviously black, and when he opened his mouth . . . my God, that voice. Like smoke and butter. He had the most majestic voice I had ever heard.

He ended up staying, smoking crack and running errands until his friend burned out and went home. By then, Sharon was over the edge. She had lost her job, the love of her life, and very nearly her sanity. She was so deep in debt she could never get out. She was exhausted and paranoid from the continuous blasts. There's no comfort in the pipe, just the soul-crushing anguish at the other end of the hit, and the pressing need for more. I was floundering, too, trying to kill myself in the pipe, but Sharon . . . she told me later she stood on our eighth-floor balcony every day, in tears, wishing for the strength to take a header to the ground.

In the end, she called her mother, who took her home.

That left me alone in the apartment. No food, no furniture, no friends. I couldn't pay the rent. I couldn't pay for crack. I didn't have anywhere else to go. I had no money. No job. I had pawned all David's prized possessions for dope, including his beloved

My momma loved me from the moment she saw me in the newborn room at St. Mary's Hospital.

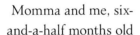

Momma and me, six-and-a-half months old

Momma met Daddy in Harlem, and within a few weeks Daddy was taking Momma to the Savoy and the Apollo.

My third birthday
party

Momma dressed
me in nice shorts
and high socks,
imitating the
Kennedy kids.

Me in my
choirboy outfit

Momma and me, Easter 1965

My daddy loved sports…but I loved entertainers.

Momma and me at the World's Fair, 1964

Three years after this was taken, I defied my father and joined the army, breaking my mother's heart.

My family in 1984: (left to right) Patty, Tangela, me, Tricia, Julia, and Jenay (front)

Patty and me, shortly after starting my job at WZZT

Momma visiting me in Columbus, Ohio, in 1985, at the height of my success as a DJ. Little did we suspect that within five years I'd be unemployed and homeless.

Definitely not some of my better days

My girlfriend, Kathy, in her younger days

My girlfriend, Kathy, with her brother and sister

Kathy and me in late 2011

I didn't want to just ask for money or write the same thing on my sign as everyone else. I wanted drivers to see me, to know me, so they understood they were giving to a real human being, someone with his own past, dreams, and, obviously, failures. I needed people to know that I had a gift, a true, honest gift that made me worthwhile: my voice.

Doral and me. Doral took the video of me that changed my life. I owe this guy a lot.

Smiling in late 2011 with my lawyer, Bret Adams, and Eric, the friend who keeps me sober

After twenty years of grinding homelessness, finally using my God-given gift in the *Today* show studio

Don't give up. Don't ever give up, because a miracle happened. A change came into my heart—that was the miracle—and if my broken addict's heart can change, then salvation is within anybody's grasp.

drums, and my family wouldn't take me back. Even if they would have, I didn't have the strength to ask. I was paralyzed with fear. I heard voices in the walls, scraping sounds in the halls, people walking back and forth, back and forth, looking for crack. I sat in the middle of the floor, staring at the door. And just when I was about to lose my mind, Ted came.

Each night, as darkness descended, he knocked on my door with a handful of rocks. We smoked until morning while I talked about my brother. Ted smoked, he listened, and occasionally he dropped that lovely voice into the silence of my heart. Then he disappeared. Every morning, when the sun came up, Ted left me. But he always came back.

After a week, he said, "I want you, Kathy." His voice was quiet, and oh-so smooth. "I saw you getting in the shower a few days ago, and I can't stop thinking about you."

I wouldn't say I was his after that. Making love was nothing but a marker. I fell in love with him, I think, because he didn't want me that way. He didn't see a sex object. He saw a person in need. And he listened. He cared. He was there for me, when no one else was—when no one else, my whole life, had ever been there. Nobody but my brother. I didn't know he was poor. I had no idea he was homeless. I just knew he was kind. He picked me up more gently than any man ever had. On those lonely, terrible nights, he was my emotional support. I knew, even then, I would never let him go.

CHAPTER 13

Kathy was an addict. That's the first thing I noticed about her. She needed her drugs and she was tenacious about getting them. I didn't know she was mourning, at least not at first. I didn't know she was spiraling. I just knew she *wanted*. No matter how much she smoked, she wanted more. That's the hard truth of crack cocaine addiction: one hit is too many, a thousand is never enough.

I assumed she was a prostitute. What other relationship could there be? My friend was an upstanding citizen with a business and a family. I'd known him for a few years, and this wasn't his scene. Until that moment, in fact, I didn't even know he smoked. And now here he was, high in the projects, thousands of dollars into a crack spree with a white hooker, clearly out of his depth. He was buying Kathy eight ball after eight ball, at $150 a pop, and he wasn't getting anything in return, not even what he could walk down the hall and get in half a second for a twenty-dollar bill.

It made me angry. It worked on my mind, seeing my friend taken like that—even though I was hanging around, smoking his dope, too. He might have been fooled, but I knew better how to treat a hooker, so two days after I arrived, when my friend stepped out for a minute, I told Kathy in no uncertain terms that she better deliver on her promises or the party was over.

She just stared at me, didn't say a word. But when my friend came back, she told him she was ready to go. He waved her away. He wasn't interested. He just wanted a quiet place to smoke, away from a crowd, because he was a weekend warrior, you know, had been nursing an occasional habit for years.

So if he didn't want Kathy . . . well, what about me? She was a gorgeous woman, blue eyes, nice body, attractive attitude, and I mean that sincerely. She was hungry and fierce and, I don't know, once I got past the issue with my friend, that fierceness turned me on.

And she was white. I mean, my daddy might have talked about them all the time, but I'd never been with a white woman. I'd never even been around one so young and fresh, because all the white women down in the hood were skeezers, as we called them, women who'd been ruined by drugs. I didn't know Kathy's brother had just died, because she kept that inside for a while. I didn't know how alone and vulnerable his death made her feel. I just knew she needed . . . something. She seemed like a woman used to lying back for a man, then watching him walk out the door. I wanted to show her I was different, that I could put feelings into it. I had this idea about white women, that you had to love them right the first time. In my mind, a black woman would give you a second chance. And a third. And even a tenth. A black woman always gave in to a little kindness, no matter what you'd done the day before. That's how I'd kept Patty and Lisa so long. A white woman gives you one chance, and if you don't love her right, she's out the door.

But if you loved her right the first time . . . she was yours.

So I took it slow. Even after my friend went home, I stayed with

Kathy, listening to her talk most of the night. In the morning, I walked to Master Ray's karate studio, where I worked the phone. Master Ray loved me because my voice attracted students. I talked a lot of people into the power, discipline, and self-respect that karate could provide. And I worked cheap. He paid me a hundred dollars cash at the end of every day, and every day I walked back to Kathy with the crack that money bought. It was a five-mile walk, one way, and I wouldn't arrive until dark. But I didn't care. I was used to hustling.

Eventually, I couldn't stand it anymore. I touched her arm, late in the night, and said, "Baby, I promise you, if you give me a chance, you will be satisfied."

She looked at me hungry, like she did the pipe. I touched her soft, like I always touched women, and before I knew it, she was naked and we were making love.

I left that morning when the sun came up, and I stayed away for three days. By the time I came back, Kathy was frantic. She didn't have anybody, and she thought I had left for good. Once I saw that look in her eye, that hunger, I knew she was mine. When the eviction notice arrived a few weeks later, there wasn't any question of taking her with me.

"You might as well sell it," I told her, "because the brothers are going to pay."

I don't want you to think I turned Kathy onto the street. Kathy made plenty of choices that had nothing to do with me. When her sister-in-law, Sharon, left, she begged Kathy to come with her and get clean, but Kathy wouldn't go. This was a few days after I'd met her, before we'd even made love. Later, sure, I was her excuse. She clung to me like a brother in those years, like no black woman ever would. But when she chose to stay in that apartment without her sister-in-law, it wasn't me she was choosing, it was crack; and after she made that choice, there wasn't anywhere to go but the street.

So I taught her the basics of the life: how to negotiate, how to sell it, how to walk. She had a pretty little walk, on her toes with her shoulders back. It was so preppy, she looked like the target of a purse snatching. I showed her how to loosen her arms and swing her hips, the so-called ho stroll. She took it around downtown a few times, and once we were evicted, we walked together down to the real ghetto, Champion and Main, my old neighborhood on the east side. I sat on the steps of the church at the corner of Bryden Road, and Kathy walked. Halfway down the block, a car pulled over and picked her up. Five minutes later, she came running around the corner.

"I got fifty dollars," she said, showing me the money. She was so proud of herself, like a kid on Christmas.

"Well, let's go," I said.

I took her to a crack house, and we bought a big rock at a good price. That was my role in the partnership, to maximize the money, because Kathy had never been on the streets. She was a home smoker; she'd never even seen the inside of a crack house. Up until a few weeks before I met her, she'd didn't even buy from the brothers on the corner, she drove out to the suburbs and bought crack twice as expensive from some white boys.

Main Street was a different life. It was a different world than sitting up in an apartment with a friend handing you the pipe. On the street, you had to hustle. It wasn't just finding the crack houses, which was a chore in itself. Crack had exploded in Columbus in the early 1990s, and there was a full-fledged war on between the dealers and the cops. Crack busts were heating up, and crack houses moved all the time, trying to outflank the undercovers and the drug squad. On the other hand, they were everywhere. I mean, I bet one in five houses was a crack house on Main Street in 1996. They were always run-down, but most of the houses in the area were run-down, so the only way to find them was to watch for people going in and out. Crack houses had a lot of foot traffic.

My job wasn't just finding crack, though. The real chore was finding good crack at a good price, because the drug was so hot that unscrupulous brothers were selling cut product and dangerous fakes. I used my contacts in the neighborhood, and I'd ask around: "Who's hot? Who's hot?"

"Around the corner, man," someone would say, their eyes lighting up, thinking of that taste I'd give them in return. "I'll take you there."

We'd find the house. Either the crack addict, who was probably inside ten minutes ago, would get us in, or I'd knock on the door, already feeling that tingle, because the anticipation was its own high. A dope boy, often about thirteen years old, would crack the door, or maybe slide open a metal slot like on television.

"What's happening, man?"

They'd look at me, then Kathy, and usually they didn't want anything to do with us. I was bad enough with my light skin. Kathy was too much: too young, too clean, too fresh. And way too white. I'm not saying white people didn't smoke crack, because they did. They just didn't come down to the crack houses on Main Street. A girl like Kathy wasn't welcome there, because a pretty white girl was too much trouble if she got hurt or arrested or even killed. When she's a ho, and she's bruised and used, yes, that's fine, because white people will write her off then, but not when she looked like somebody's college-graduate sister.

So I'd throw my voice at them. "Hey, man, it's Radio. You heard of me, right? *Nothing but the best of yesterday's hits and today's jams.*

Your chance to win, every hour on the hour. Visit Southeast Seafood, friends, and don't forget to try the soup."

Nine out of ten times, that worked. They either knew of me or they figured I wasn't a cop, because word would have been out on my voice the first day. So they'd slide open the door with a smile and say, "Come on in, Radio, you gotta do that thing for my boy."

Pretty soon I'd be entertaining a whole house full of dealers. I'd drop jokes and Crack That Whip, *"Wha-pow,* boy, you got to shave that fade, because you're looking like Kid 'n' Play up in here," and they'd laugh and slap their knees. They were mostly teenagers, usually set up in a nasty kitchen with Chinese food on the counters or on a sofa watching television with their automatic weapons nearby. They'd offer me a bite of food or they'd break off a little piece, saying, "You're all right, Radio. Get you some extra."

Once I had that piece in my hand, I didn't want to wait. "Can I take a blast?"

"Nah, man, get out of here."

They kept the dealers and the users separate. You never smoked around the dealers, and the dealers rarely smoked at all, because they saw the consequences. They weren't my friends. They weren't any user's friends. They laughed at my jokes, sometimes they let me cook them dinner because I was pretty good with pork chops, but I didn't have illusions. I was a customer, and they didn't care if I lived or died, because there were always more customers, an almost endless supply.

On the smoky side of the house, there was more of a community. Brothers were always coming up to me, shaking my hand. A lot of them were covered with sores, peeling skin, lots of AIDS back then, but I didn't care how they looked, I'd give them a hug.

"Hey, Radio, when you getting back on the air?" They pinned

their hope on me, you see, because they didn't have any hope for themselves.

"I don't know brother, I don't know."

"You got to get up there, man. You got to share that voice." And then, because every conversation in a crack house was about crack, "Can I get a little of that rock? I'm in need."

It was like that in a crack house, a lot of activity, people energized, going in and out, looking for money or a hit. There was always someone yelling "I need a wake-up. Anybody got a wake-up?" A wake-up was the first hit of the day, but there was no day for a crack addict, no schedule, so a wake-up really meant the first hit after a nod. Usually, I was the guy to give it to them. I was a giver, always have been. Many times, I had a little piece for a brother in need.

Kathy hated that. She hated my generosity. She always said, "I worked too hard for it, Ted. I worked too hard to give it away." She wouldn't give anything away, ever, from the first day I met her.

Especially to a woman. I always had women around me in a crack house, and not just because I was generous. I was also safe. Most men wanted to trade sex for rocks, because crack addiction was a dirty business that way, but all a woman had to do was show me a little ankle, maybe touch my leg with her bare foot, and I'd give her a piece. That drove Kathy crazy. She was so jealous. She would give me sex sometimes just to drive those women away. It was the extent of our intimacy in those days.

But more than jealous, Kathy was hungry. She wanted crack, and she wanted it all the time. She was a fiend for taking out the chore, which would get full of crack resin after four or five hits, squeezing it into the tip of the pipe, and smoking it like a rock. Everybody did that. Nobody wasted. But nobody smoked chore like Kathy either; she burned that steel wool to a nub. She was smoking her head off, searching for that high, and when the money ran out, it was nothing for her to make a hundred, maybe even two hundred dollars, and we'd be back in the crack house in half an hour, with another pile to smoke. And when that was gone an hour or two later, we'd do it again.

We slept every few days, a few hours at a time. Often, we'd lay up in crack houses, crashing out on the floor. Every week or so, we'd hit the emergency room of Grant Hospital, which was across the highway from Main Street, but only two blocks away. They let you sleep in the emergency room waiting area, nobody ever bothered you. We'd wash up in their bathroom, too, especially Kathy, who had to smell respectable for the stroll.

Those breaks, though, were few. For the most part, it was smoking, smoking, smoking, day in, night out. No regrets or second thoughts. We were on a binge, and I was living large, because crack was coming faster and easier than ever before. It didn't matter if it was night or day, because there's no time on a spree, no contact with the ordinary world, just product and customer, customer and product, rock and chore and rock some more. We went from dope house to the corner and back, and for months that was our existence. It was anything we could do to get the best hit for the lowest price: duck into alleys, hit five dope houses in a row, find an addict holding, and fire up in an abandoned store. If Kathy disappeared for a while, I scraped up my own funds by stealing, but we always found each other again, and within minutes we'd be ducking into an alley for a blast.

If it bothered Kathy, the way we were living, I never noticed. We were going into places she'd never gone, doing things she'd never done, but she was a tough girl, she lost her fear—of ghetto blacks, of alleys, of rats and roaches and filthy toilets and whatever else might have bothered her once upon a time. I never asked what she had to do for the money, and she never told me, so it was a few weeks before I realized she was ripping off johns. One night, she came running around the corner toward the church, and my heart jumped like it always did when I saw her, because I knew she had money for dope. Then I noticed the man chasing her. Kathy ran by me, I stepped in front to stop him, and he sucker punched me in the head on the dead run, knocking me unconscious. I never saw it coming.

Another dude pushed me against a wall and held a gun to my head. He hadn't gotten off, and he thought I was Kathy's pimp. I was never a pimp. I was a lover not a fighter, as Michael Jackson once said, and I immediately told Kathy to give the money back. She wouldn't, so I straight out begged that woman to give the money back. It was fifty dollars, I think, and there was no way I was getting killed for fifty dollars. But Kathy wouldn't give it up. She was always like that with money, nobody was going to take it from her.

She took a beatdown one time, a serious beatdown, from two men she tried to run on. I saw it happening and shouted for help, but the neighbors ignored me. It was that kind of neighborhood. So Kathy took the beating. She took their best shots, but she didn't give in. She was still clutching their hundred dollars in her bloody hand when they walked away in disgust. She staggered up to me, her eye already swollen, and held the money up to my face. When she smiled, there was blood on her teeth.

That's how addicted Kathy was. That's how dedicated to the drug. I was a longtime hustler, a veteran addict, so I understood the logic of the street that says don't gamble your life, because there's always more. Ted Williams was a taker and a giver, easy come, easy go. But Kathy, she was different. She never could let anything go.

Kathy

The crack houses were filthy. Nobody swept them. Nobody cleaned. They started as abandoned houses, and they got worse from there. Chore and broken glass on the floors. Discarded lighters thrown into corners. Boards over the windows. Moldy ceiling falling down on top of you. The grime an inch thick and full of dead bugs. The nicer ones had furniture, but most were temporary flops, there for a week and gone, so nobody bothered with chairs. Or electricity. Even in the nice ones, the bathrooms were unspeakable. The flies alone made me retch, and I don't want to even think about what they were eating.

I wasn't naïve. I knew I was entering a new world. The dark world, I called it; the addict's life. I knew I would be selling my body. *You have to do it*, I told myself. *If you want crack, you don't have a choice.* I thought it was a short step, like pawning my dead brother's drums or conning my friends. I was wrong. It was a long step from even my tenement world to stashing my clothes in a plastic bag in the bushes, knocking roaches off my legs while I smoked, and taking strange men into alleys.

Every woman does it, I told myself. *Every woman trades her body for what a man can provide: money, prestige, security, a home.* Hadn't I been doing it all my life?

I remember the first john. He rolled up to me. We negotiated. I got in his car. He drove around the corner and handed me fifty dollars. I looked at it . . . and jumped out. I ran, found Ted, and said, "Look what I got!" It was so easy. Fifty dollars in two minutes. I'd never made money like that.

Ted jumped right up. I could tell he was excited. He knew where to get crack, so we smoked it. Immediately. When it was gone, I said, "Let me try again."

I went out and did the same thing. I jumped and ran, this time with a hundred dollars.

The next day, a john turned right instead of left like I told him. That's when the truth hit me. I was in his car. I was at his mercy. He could do whatever he wanted. Rape me. Hurt me. I still get chills thinking about the terror. The absolute terror. Finally, he pulled over. "I'm a cop," he said. "You're under arrest."

I didn't believe him. I still thought he was going to rape me. So I punched and kicked, fighting like an animal. Of course, I was charged with resisting arrest, in addition to soliciting.

The police, though, were the least of the dangers. The johns were worse. They drove me into neighborhoods I didn't know, then attacked me. They drove into deserted areas and said, "I only got five dollars." I'd refuse and they'd throw me out. Or I'd give them what they wanted and they'd throw me out anyway. These weren't good men. Most loved being violent with women. They loved demeaning us. They got off on feeling superior, and the worse they treated me, the better they felt. They threatened me just to see me scream. They smacked me around. They said, "Twenty dollars for everything I want, bitch, that's my offer," and if I refused, they'd beat me until I bled.

I talked one guy up to a hundred dollars, but he tore me so bad, and for so long, that I finally said, "Enough."

He wanted his money back.

I said, "No," and stepped out of his car. He came after me, but I didn't care. After what he put me through, I wasn't giving it up. That money was mine. I found out later this was his shtick. He had sex with prostitutes, then beat them up. That's what he planned for me. But Ted showed up, so the man turned on him. One threat and Ted was saying, "Give the man his money, baby, just give him what he wants." Finally, I turned it loose. Not for me, but for Ted. It was a nightmare. A total nightmare. All that work for nothing.

Another time, I was walking the strip when someone grabbed me by the hair, pulled me into an alley, and slammed me against a brick wall. I looked up, blood in my mouth. It was a drug dealer I'd stiffed for twenty dollars in the tenements a month before. He pulled a gun, stuck it in my face, and said, "Bitch, I want my money, and I want it now."

I started shaking. If I had the money I'd have given it to him, but I'd smoked every dime. I said, "What can I do?"

He pistol-whipped me and broke my lip.

I said, "I'll bring you twenty dollars. I'll bring forty for making you wait."

He pistol-whipped me again, putting a bruise across my cheek.

"You know where I am," I said. "You know I smoke. I'm not going anywhere."

He kept me pinned against the wall, choking me. No matter what I said it wasn't enough. He wasn't going to let me go. Finally, I said, "Just shoot me, then. My life isn't worth twenty dollars anyway."

It was defiant. A challenge. I didn't want to die, but I sure as hell didn't want to stay there either, and the only way out was to fight. He knew I was serious. I guess he could see it. He dropped me to the ground and hovered over me, but as soon as I caught my breath, I pushed him away. I tottered off in my high heels without looking back. Eventually, I paid him. What else could I do? He knew where I was. He wasn't going away.

A few weeks later I got in a car with a john. He drove a few blocks, smiled, and said, "Remember me?"

I didn't. They were all the same.

He took me to a secluded spot, grabbed my hair, and put a knife to my throat. He said, "You took me for five dollars, bitch. Now I want what's mine." He busted me in the mouth. He punched me in the head repeatedly until I saw stars. I couldn't get away. I was screaming, but he knew where to take me, there was no one around. He pointed the knife at my eye. "You're mine."

That's when I got desperate. I was about to pass out, and he was going to kill me, by accident if nothing else.

I stopped fighting. "I'll give you what you want. Anything you want."

He put the car in drive. "I'm taking you home, bitch."

He was doing forty miles an hour when I jumped. Or rather, I tried to jump, but he grabbed my hair. I was hanging out the door, struggling to pull myself away, and then, just as I was breaking free, he shoved me out. I took a dive into the pavement, busted my head open, and bounced into a gravel ditch. I couldn't get up. I couldn't move. I know I had a concussion, maybe a busted skull, but I never went to the doctor. I lay on the side of the road, staring into the darkness, until a man picked me up. I couldn't see him. I couldn't speak. I felt his hands lift me, my vision swung around, and pain drove so deep into my skull that I blacked out.

He took me to his house. He fed me. He let me sleep in his bed while he nursed me for three days. It wasn't innocent. Of course. I had to have sex with him in exchange for the food and the bed or he wouldn't let me leave.

So I did. I let him use me. Then I staggered back to Ted and never told him what happened. Even though I was gone three days, and had no money, only two black eyes, he never asked. He took me in, gave me a hit, and an hour later I was back on the street.

I thought, *I gotta change. I gotta smarten up or I'm gonna die.*

CHAPTER 14

didn't think we'd make it six months. I don't mean our relationship, which I figured would end any day. I mean, the way we were going, I didn't think we'd live for a year. You just can't survive like that for long, smoking night and day, no place to lay your head. I thought an angry john, or another whore, or even a junkie, would take Kathy out. She had developed a hard attitude, a don't-care disposition, where she didn't take anything from anybody. She never backed down from a fight, and that's the kind of thing that gets you killed.

It was Lieutenant Price, though, who finally drove us out of the neighborhood. Every whore, black or white, knew Price in Vice, because he was a hard cop. He'd arrest you for loitering on the wrong park bench, because he knew you were homeless and vagrancy was a crime. But Kathy didn't get it, she never figured him out. He'd wear a fake mustache and switch cars, and she'd fall for it again. I think he arrested her five times in two months and sent her to city jail twice. He wouldn't leave her alone, and Kathy couldn't learn.

So we moved east on Main Street a few miles to a mixed working class neighborhood where I'd lived on and off for years. Master Ray's karate studio was there, so I got my old job back soliciting for karate students, and we moved into Master Ray's storage room. There's a give and flow to homelessness. You can't run all the time, you need a place to rest. I must have come back to Master Ray eight or nine times over the years, and no matter what I'd done the last time, he always took me back.

You probably don't understand that, an honest businessman taking in a homeless addict. It probably seems like more trouble than it's worth. And maybe it is, I don't know. But you have to understand, in the urban black community, even in 1997, crack was still a major part of life. It wasn't an epidemic anymore, but the remnants of the crack boom, the crackheads, were everywhere, so the tax-paying citizens had to make a decision. You could ignore them and they'd probably ignore you. Lots of people, like my mother, resented them. She hates homeless people and drug addicts. To her, they're worse than nothing. They ruin the neighborhood, destroy families, and embarrass the race. It wasn't just her family she lost to drugs, it was her beloved Bed-Stuy, where back in the day she could go down to the club and listen to jazz with her husband in peace. Even today, she'll give a homeless person the cold shoulder, but she'd never give a handout, and I understand why. It's too personal. And besides, she's given enough to me.

Many people, though, went the other way. And it wasn't just church members either, the ones touched by God's love in their hearts. Black folks, on the whole, are a generous people. Many don't have much, but they've earned what they got. They have faced bigotry and discrimination. They have lived in struggling neighborhoods. They saw the crack epidemic firsthand and the devastation it left. They understand the importance of helping their own.

Some, like my friend Eric from the Salvation Army, had been addicted themselves. Others had lost loved ones. Still others, like Master Ray, simply saw an opportunity to help. We had met through my cousin, who was his karate student, during my second chance at WJZA in 1996. We talked about cutting a few commercials, he liked me, and we became friends. When I lost my radio job, I asked if he'd hire me. He knew I had a crack problem, that was no secret, but he took me in.

He told me, "I'm going to teach you discipline, Ted. That's gonna be part of it, too."

He didn't try to stop my habit, because that don't work. You can't withhold a person out of addiction. He made me take karate lessons, just him and me, sometimes for hours at a time. I mean, Master Ray wore my butt out. I didn't earn any belts because it was informal training, but I learned a few moves, and I learned to be humble in my heart, because my chest, you know, it was killing me. I could hardly breathe.

He beat me up a few times, too, when I stole from him. He didn't hurt me physically, because that would have been too easy. Master Ray wasn't one of those skinny karate dudes. He was a giant—he's got two sons playing NFL football right now, and he's bigger than they are—and an eighth-degree black belt, so he could have broken me in half.

He beat me up psychologically: lectured me, docked my pay, increased my required exercise. He told me, "Look, Ted, you can't be biting the hand that feeds you. I'm trying to be nice to you here."

"Yes, sensei," I'd say, because he was my master and I was his pupil. The worst pupil he ever had, but still.

The first time, the exercise was jogging. Then squats. After I relapsed and hooked up with Kathy, it was push-ups. Every day, when I came out of the storage closet, Master Ray said, "Give me ten, Ted."

Actually, that was later. The first day, he said, "Let me see you do ten, Ted," and I got down in the forward lean, push-up position,

and just about passed out. I couldn't even do two. So we started
with two, worked our way up. When I made it to ten, Master Ray
laughed and said, "Knuckle push-ups, Ted. Let me see you do two."

I got on my knuckles and collapsed straight to the floor, because
muscle weakness was one thing, but pain was another. I've never
taken well to pain.

Master Ray shook his head. "Discipline, Ted. You got to put your
mind to it."

It wasn't cruelty. He wasn't picking on me. Master Ray liked me,
and he liked having me around. I was a personable guy. I always
had a smile for everyone, always had a laugh, never forgot a face.
During the day, usually noon to eight, I worked the phone, selling
mothers on karate lessons for their kids.

"It's about discipline, ma'am. It's about getting strong, mentally
and physically."

I was good at it. I brought in a lot of students.

At night, I swept the dojo, cleaned the bathroom, answered the
late calls. Master Ray knew I was stealing here and there, because
I had the sickness, and I couldn't feed it on a hundred dollars a day,
but I was earning my keep, and it was a good deal for everyone.
Kathy and I had a shower. We had a roof over our heads. Kathy had
white country bars she could walk to for tricks, where she didn't
have to worry so much about being beat up. We even had a dealer
who delivered dope right to Master Ray's back door.

But I never thought it was permanent. We couldn't live in Master Ray's closet forever. And there was never any thought of getting
out of the life. The better you were living, the more chances you
had to clean up, but why would you when everything was so easy,
and you could smoke a hundred dollars of crack a day (even more
when Kathy was hooking) in the comforts of a storage room?

But a hundred dollars wouldn't do it after a while, not because we built up a tolerance, that never happened—my ten thousandth hit was as good as my tenth—but because we built up a hunger. After a while, four hours a day of being high wasn't enough. And pretty soon eight hours wasn't enough either. I don't want to put it on Kathy, but I could be satisfied if I could smoke for a few hours and stop, but she always wanted more. Whatever she smoked, it was never enough.

In the end, the pressure of our habits got to me. Or maybe it was the temptation. I was on the phone selling yearly karate contracts almost every day, and I knew some of those people stopped coming long before their contracts were up. Master Ray kept a file on delinquent payments, but he never personally checked them, he only sent them to a collection agency every once in a while. So I got the file, and whenever Master Ray was out of the studio, I called names on the list.

"I see you owe five hundred dollars to Master Ray for karate lessons, Mrs. Smith. I got the paperwork right here. Now . . . I know these payments are hard. I know your kid don't want to do it anymore. So I'll tell you what. If you come down to the studio right now and give me a hundred dollars in cash, I'll tear that contract up."

I was tearing up a lot of contracts and collecting a lot of cash. I was making more cash off that scam than my job and Kathy's hooking combined, and the more I made, the more Kathy and I smoked. But of course it was just another way of stealing from Master Ray, since he was owed that money; and after a few months he figured out what was going on. The collection agency called a few people, and they said, "Oh no, I straightened that out at the studio. Paid up and got my contract back. Paid who? Oh, that guy with the radio voice."

By then, though, Kathy and I were gone. Discipline, indeed.

Kathy

My family blames Ted for putting me on the street. That's fine. I understand. They need someone to blame. Everybody does. But in reality, Ted saved me. He cared for me. He knew the dark world, and he knew how to work the system. He had friends. He could charm anyone. His big personality, that radio voice, could get us out of any jam.

Then he went to prison for a few months and I was on my own. Suddenly, they wouldn't let me in the crack house. Even some of the corner dealers wouldn't sell me dope. I had to hunt around. I must have gotten ripped off five times before I finally scored at a moldy, ant-infested crack house. I went into a back room and sat alone in the dark. I could feel the place crawling. I hit the pipe fast, just to kill the dread. I'd never felt so small and lost.

You gotta get help, Kathy. You gotta get help.

There were a group of girls in the house. They were prostitutes. I recognized them from the street, but I knew better than to trust them just because they were women. In Davey's tenement building, there was an eighteen-year-old, eight-month-pregnant girl turning twenty-dollar tricks for crack. I saw her walk into a room, then walk out with a rock, over and over again for days. I couldn't stand it. I told her I'd take her away, pay somehow to set her up in a nice place with her baby. She took my money, but kept turning tricks and smoking crack, poisoning her own child. That's the street. Everybody is dope sick. Everyone is out for themselves.

But I couldn't see another choice. I needed protection. I needed to learn the business. And I knew the main girl, Sarah, was one of the best. She was young, but she'd been on the streets for years. She had a boyfriend who was a dealer, and the two of them were well known. He died a few years later when he swallowed a bag of crack during a traffic stop. I don't know what happened to her. She loved him, but she was a pro. She was hard. That day in the crack house, she saw me for exactly who I was, a moneymaker, and she stripped my innocence down.

She took me out of the house. (After smoking my rock.) She set me up in a motel. (I paid for the room.) She denied me crack. (I paid for that, too.) She smoked it in front of me until I was so hungry for it, I agreed to have sex with her. When that didn't work out, because I was disgusted, she said, "Pick up a john. I'll show you how to work a motel room."

I did. I brought him back, and she offered him two for one. While I kept him busy, she rifled his clothes. She stole his money, his credit card, even his wedding ring. I could see it happening. She was right in the room. She didn't even look at me when she walked out. She just closed the door. I had to duck out later, while he was naked on the bed. She wasn't even waiting, because she didn't care what happened to me. She got what she came for.

I went back to her anyway. Where else could I go? We ran the motel scam for weeks. I went through the motions, she went through the clothes. She knew I wasn't interested in sex, with a man or a woman, but I was a talker. I could keep a john occupied. She did the rest. She taught me how to kite checks, using straw men to cash them at businesses that didn't check identification. She taught me to peek into the man's wallet and coax him to an ATM machine, then memorize his PIN number. She could withdraw a thousand dollars in minutes, or take a credit card to the gas station for a dozen cartons of cigarettes before the man knew it was gone.

Eventually, she pimped me out. She asked a hundred dollars for an introduction, was paid up front, and never told me. I never saw a penny. She convinced johns to take us home solely on the promise of my clean white body. Then she rummaged their drawers for jewelry, collectibles, bank statements, and checkbooks while I kept them occupied. That was scary, because I was always the woman left behind. If I was caught, prison was the best I could hope for. A bad beating was more likely. Death wasn't out of the question, because these were scary men. But they never caught us. We made thousands of dollars a week, more than I could have made on the corner in a month. I barely saw any of it.

But I gained knowledge. I saw how the dark world worked. This was the real game, I realized. And if I played it well, it would keep me alive.

CHAPTER 15

We moved about a mile away from Master Ray's studio to a motel near Interstate 71. We were cycling into the beginning of a spree, not yet blasted all day on crack, so we still had money for a room and the mind-set to get more.

It was November 1996, Thanksgiving and Christmas around the corner, the best time of the year. The weather wasn't good, but the feeling in the air! Everybody wants something for Christmas. Want, want, want. So there's no end to what a smart thief can make since it's never the stealing that's the primary problem but the selling on the other end. At Christmastime, I hit the nearby Toys"R"Us store every few days for weeks, stealing as much as I could safely shove into my coat. Then I walked fifteen minutes to the bar area across the interstate and sold the toys to the highest bidder.

Soon, I was taking orders. *My son is into Power Rangers. My daughter wants Barbie. Not that Barbie, the one with the car.*

There was a department store a short walk from the motel, where I stole jackets for men and perfume for their wives. If something sold well, I stole more. Electronics were popular, especially cell phones, which were pretty new back then, pretty expensive, and easy to shove in a pocket. I'd walk out of Walmart with two hundred dollars in merchandise under my coat, and I'd steal a fifty-cent candy bar on the way out, my only meal.

Meanwhile, Kathy worked the bars. She had a way of eyeing a room and figuring out who wanted companionship bad enough to pay. Then she'd talk them into it. She could go into a bar and walk out with a guy in fifteen minutes, bring him back to the motel, and rob him blind. I'm not kidding, she'd go into a motel room for thirty seconds, walk out with a hundred dollars, and never go back. She was the best talker I've ever known.

It wasn't long before I was involved. She'd introduce me as her brother, and believe me, most of those guys weren't happy to see me, even though I didn't look like a heavy. Throw a man in the mix, any man, and hooker sex gets scary fast, especially if you're a husband or father on a spur-of-the-moment idea. But I soothed them with my voice, started a friendly conversation, and by the time they paid their money and walked into that hotel room, Kathy had lifted their credit card. I'd run to the gas station and buy a bunch of gas cards, which were almost as good as cash on the black market, and I'd still be back in time to slip the credit card into his pocket.

Or Kathy would step out of the room for ice and slip me a bank card, because she was great at scoping PINs. She couldn't remember Lieutenant Price from Vice to save her life, but she remembered those numbers. She'd give me the card, and I'd withdraw the maximum. Then I'd knock on the door to let her know I was done.

"Hey, what are you doing with my sister in there?"

Kathy always came to the door. "Just a minute, brother," exasperated-sounding, and I'd slip her the card. She'd come out a minute later, fully dressed, and 90 percent of the time she hadn't even performed. That was the most amazing part of the scam.

She'd talk to them and tease them and then, wham, she was gone, without giving them what they paid for.

It wasn't long, though, before she'd pick up the same man again. Kathy was terrible about that. I knew every customer that ever bought deodorant from me, but Kathy could never remember a face.

They said, "You stiffed me, bitch."

She said, "Then come back to the motel with me."

And she'd do it to them again! She took the same guys three, four times, for hundreds of dollars, without ever giving them anything; and God help me, it's a sin, but I loved her for it. She was a great partner, a real hustler and earner like me, and between the two of us the sky was the limit. We were pulling down hundreds of dollars a day, and we smoked it all.

I felt so good about my life, in fact, I decided to visit my kids for Christmas. I had a little money and some stolen toys, so I thought I was rolling. I thought I could be a father again, at least for a day. Patty wasn't happy with the idea. We both knew there was no hope of my coming back, so it was easier to have me out of their lives completely. But Patty tolerated me . . . again . . . until I showed up a day late, high as a kite and reeking of the street. I had no idea of my condition. I was all smiles when Patty opened her door. It wasn't until I saw the look in my children's eyes that I understood what a disgrace I'd become.

It wasn't any better when I got back to the motel. Kathy yelled at me, saying I wasted my time and her money. I think she was jealous, because in my delusion I told her, "Those are my children, and my children come first."

"What about me? I'm your woman. I'm the one selling my body for you."

"I make my own money. I don't need you."

It was true. We didn't need each other, not for money anyway, but we depended on each other. Codependent, they called it in rehab. We fed each other's habits, gave each other a reason. We fought like crazy sometimes—you can't run a business with someone and be their lover and have mountains of crack between you without fighting. She'd call me names, trying to bring out the monster in me, and pretty soon we'd be hollering and shoving and Kathy would threaten to call the police. But she never did, not in our whole time together, because we had crack paraphernalia and outstanding warrants. Nothing good could come of it, and what did she want to lose me for anyway? Why would she want to see me taken away in irons?

Eventually, the motel kicked us out, both for soliciting and fighting. By then it was edging toward spring, and we had a spot in the forest picked out. I'd found it one night when I was looking for a shortcut from our crack house to the motel. I was bushwhacking through scraggly trees and bushes, cursing my adventurous spirit, when suddenly I came across a nice flat area. It had bushes all around, blocking it from view, and a nice place to stretch out. It even had a little stream, although it wasn't really a stream, it was a drainage ditch. We started stopping there on the way home for a blast, and it became Kathy's bathroom spot. She was a clean freak, she was really into hygiene, and you know that crack house bathroom must have been nasty if she preferred relieving herself in the forest. When the motel finally got around to booting us out, we stole the pillows and sheets and spread out on the ground.

It was a simple setup because dope fiends like to keep it simple. We didn't even have a tent. We had two buckets, one for a toilet and one for washing, because Kathy was serious about keeping clean. I just rubbed toothpaste in my mouth with a finger, but

Kathy always kept a toothbrush. I let my Afro go, but she combed her hair. I rarely washed. She cleaned herself every day. I went without underpants and threw my shirts out when they got dirty, because there was always a Salvation Army drop box to rifle through or a charity giving out clean clothes. If you ever see a filthy homeless person, that person is sick or crazy, because no matter how bad your addictions, there's no need to dress like a bum. Kathy, meanwhile, washed her underthings. We'd stay up all night hitting the pipe, while her socks and panties hung off tree branches all around us like white ghosts. Especially socks, Kathy was fanatical about clean socks. She even went to the Laundromat to wash out her dresses, which she kept in a plastic bag. I didn't complain about the wasted crack money. Cleanliness was good for business. You don't want to be reeking like a homeless person when you're selling sex— or at least the promise of sex because, like I said, Kathy was a con artist, and very few got what they paid for.

Without the motel, we narrowed our world. We stopped walking for work and focused on the shift changes at the nearby factory. Kathy sold promises, I sold stolen goods, on order or buyer's choice. From there it was two blocks to the crack house. Then another block to the gas stations along Hamilton Road, where we bought gas cards and stole toilet paper. Every bathroom we went into, we stole the toilet paper.

When it rained, we simply let it come down on our heads. Mostly it was just a sprinkle under all those trees, but there were nights when we huddled in hoodies, trying to light a pipe with shaking hands in the pouring rain. Once the pipe was lit, of course, it wasn't so bad, and even the anticipation, the physical rush when the crack was in the pipe, was enough to see me through most storms. When the weather got too bad, we'd run under an awning, or spend a few extra hours in the crack house, or duck into a gas station to get warm. Sometimes, soaked to the bone, we'd hold each other, sharing our body heat, until the worst of it passed. Afterward, I'd sneak back to the motel and steal dry sheets and pillows off the maid's cart, maybe soap and shampoo if Kathy needed fresh supplies.

That's what happens on a binge. The world gets small. Your life becomes a hustle for the next twenty dollars, the smallest amount I'd take to a dealer. Most dealers would sell ten-dollar pieces, or even fives, but that was for junkies and crumb-buyers, people who couldn't get a real stake together. A twenty-dollar piece was a respectable chunk, a high worth hustling for. When money got tight, I sometimes took fifteen dollars, and because I had such a good relationship with the dealers, they gave me twenty dollars' worth anyway, but that didn't happen much. It wasn't hard for us to get twenty together, five or six times a day, between the shoplifting and the tricks.

The only problem with our campsite, really, was the noise. The forest was just a strip of trees, bordered on two sides by roads, so there was always traffic. There were overhead wires and sometimes, late at night, I heard voices from the nearby neighborhood or behind us in the direction of the motel. Crack doesn't make you hallucinate, you never see things that aren't there, but it does heighten your senses, and it makes you paranoid as hell. I'd sit out in the woods with the pipe in my hand, following the drift of unseen conversations, listening to the police cars screaming by, knowing that eventually someone was going to find our camp.

Then one night I heard it. I was taking a blast, staring up at Kathy's socks waving like ghosts in the trees, when I heard a short, hard sound, like a laugh in the woods. Or maybe a signal. I lowered the pipe and held my breath, listening, and sure enough, I heard the crunch of leaves underfoot, coming closer. I blew out the blast and buried the pipe under my sheets, my chest getting tighter and tighter, my ears bugging until I could hear a slow breathing, in and out, somewhere in the dark. It wasn't cops, because they'd never sneak. It had to be thieves, maybe teens looking for someone to beat up, maybe other homeless stumbling out of the crack house, seeing my lighter in the dark. I sat still, listening. The socks fluttered. The traffic hummed by in the distance. I heard the branches parting behind me, I heard the deep breathing.

I jumped. I turned into the darkness, ready to fight, and saw two big brown eyes staring at me from two feet away. I stumbled back, looked to the left, and there were two more, and two more beyond that.

"What is it?" Kathy mumbled, sitting up.

"Run," I said.

"What?"

"Just run."

We didn't grab our pipes. We didn't grab our sheets or even our clothes. We beat it out of the forest so fast, plowing through vines and bushes, that I was out of breath by the time we hit the motel parking lot.

"What was that?" Kathy said, huffing beside me.

I bent down to catch my breath.

"What was that?" Kathy asked, frantic.

"Deer," I said, wheezing badly. "A herd of d*mn deer."

Kathy

I know it sounds hard, living in the forest beside a drainage ditch. No washing machine. No cups or plates. No cover against the rain. Nothing but a bucket for your business and a gas station bathroom for your shower.

It wasn't hard, though, not compared to how we'd been living. Those first six months, we were always running. Our life was crowded. Drug dealers, cops, addicts, the greedy hands of the crack house crowd. I wanted to slink off and get high with my man, but Ted was always in the corner with a woman's foot on his knee, or making a group of addicts laugh with his radio routines.

At the motel, it was worse. There were a dozen hookers working out of that place, so it was always a hustle. I was in the bar picking up men, or in the parking lot waiting for them to give me the eye. I had a 98 percent rule. If a man hired me, 98 percent of the time he wasn't getting sex. Because the sex made me sick. So I never thought about it. I thought, *I'm getting the money, then I'm getting out.* But that was a grind, a constant hustle. In and out of rooms. In and out of compromising situations with strange men, always on the lookout against the next opportunity or knife to the throat.

A blind john, for instance, was dealing drugs out of the motel. It was almost a party, girls coming and going, and one night I got a look at the money. It was thousands of dollars, and to me that meant months of the easy life with Ted, just waiting for the taking. Well, he caught me. He heard me in the drawer, and he called his people. Three women. Mean women. They ripped my clothes off looking for that money. They beat my face and took a leather strap to my back. I walked out of that room with blood on my face, blood on my arms, my one functioning hand holding my torn dress over my chest.

But I got the money. Several hundred dollars, hidden in my sock. I walked out of rooms bloody and beaten plenty of times with less. That was the life. Some guys caught me cheating them. Others just liked to smack women around. I don't know how many times I've been raped. One hundred at least, probably more. A lot more. There were times on the street . . . there were whole years when I was convinced that everyone—every single person—was out to hurt me.

Except Ted. I never worried about Ted. Sometimes we argued. Sometimes he slapped my face. He had his moments, because he was a crack addict like me, but he never wanted to hurt me. He was gentle in a way no other man had been for a long time. He had a kind soul. He laughed all the time. I hated his generosity, the way he never turned away a user, especially a woman, but I loved that about him, too, that he never lost his spirit.

Ted wasn't hard. He wasn't cold. When I lay with him alone in the forest, I felt at peace. I could unburden myself. After a while, it became almost a compulsion to tell him what I had done in those seedy motel rooms. He didn't hug me. He didn't say it was okay. He didn't thank me. He never, not to this day, said he loved me.

But he didn't turn away from me either. He didn't hate me for it. He didn't treat me like my family did, on the rare occasions that I saw them: like I was disgusting. Like I had some kind of contagious disease.

And somehow, that made it okay. When I laid up in the forest with Ted, away from all the other broken people that inhabited our life, I felt good about myself. I felt almost . . . happy. Content. Even safe. As long as I had Ted, and enough crack to stay high ten hours a day, I could survive the rest.

CHAPTER 16

We moved further out on Main Street, past the loop highway that circles urban Columbus, and started the cycle again. Homelessness is a process of stripping away, first your basic needs—*I don't need a dresser to keep my shirts in. I don't need a pot for cooking. I don't need clean clothes. I don't need to eat every day*—then your ambitions and desires, and finally your hope. Some people lose their minds out there, but I never went that far. I knew who I was, and I knew what I was doing, but I was a shell of my old self. It had been nine years since my first hit in 1988, and most days there wasn't a thought in my head except finding a way to smoke the next rock.

In the past, when I was dreaming of Lisa, I'd always thought, *This is temporary. I'm going to make it back.* Sometimes I'd sit in the crack house and think, *This is my last rock*, or *This is my last day smoking.* Never happened, but the thought—the desire—was there.

After I met Kathy, things changed, although it wasn't Kathy's fault. She happened to come along just after my terminal relapse, when I threw away my dreams. I'd lost Lisa, who had inspired me to get clean so many times. I'd lost my children. I'd blown my last chance at radio, because nobody was going to take me back after Horace Perkins, and without radio, who was I? Nobody. What was I going back to? Nothing.

I called my momma every now and then, and she told me, "Come home, Ted. You have a home here, come home. But you've got to come home alone."

I couldn't do it. I couldn't leave the drugs. And I couldn't leave Kathy. She was my partner. She inspired me with her take-no-prisoners attitude, she fed me, she kept me from the terminal loneliness of the street. I was never a homeless man with homeless friends. I was civil, even spending a day or two with my fellow users sometimes, especially if there was dope. But I never connected. It was always a meeting of convenience, a false front of hugs and radio jokes, with an eye for the open door. If anybody says they ran with Ted Williams, they're lying, because Ted Williams was a loner. I only ran with Kathy. There wasn't much sex, almost none in fact, and sometimes there wasn't even much talking. But seeing Kathy walking out of a motel room in her fishnet stockings with two hundred dollars in crack money in her hand *for doing nothing, nothing at all*, lit my fire.

Bonnie and Clyde, that's what we were. We didn't have guns or a car, but we were on a crime spree for years. We were the turtle, you know, slow and steady wins the race, a little every day instead of a lot, but we didn't realize we were racing to the bottom. We thought we were living. We were homeless, sure, because we didn't have an apartment, we didn't have legitimate jobs, we didn't have welfare or social security or even identification. We were outside the system, living by our wits. We stayed indoors most of the time, usually crashing with old friends of mine. Master Ray took us in, although our stays seemed shorter each time. I voiced radio commercials for my promoter friend Al Battle, whenever he could find me. We lived with my friend Eric from the Salvation Army on and off for three years, until I found almost a thousand dollars stashed in his closet and disappeared with it, along with most of his shoes.

Kathy, meanwhile, started looking for men to take her in. At first, it was meals and showers, staying at their houses for a day so she could clean up and eat. She'd disappear for a few days, and I knew she was working. She never did anything else. Eventually, she'd call and tell me where to meet her. She'd tell the john I was her brother. We'd live with them for a few days, conning them out of meals and gifts and stealing little things they wouldn't notice, like old stereo equipment or receipts. We'd take the receipt to the store, grab the item off the shelf, and return it for cash, showing the receipt as proof of purchase. I invented that con, and it worked perfectly, since who was going to miss a receipt?

Eventually, it would fall apart. They'd kick us out, or we'd get bored and steal their credit card. There was never any plan, just a crime of opportunity. Usually, the score was a few hundred dollars, but even when it was a thousand, we never saved a dime. Maybe we'd rent a motel room for a week, or Kathy would buy new clothes for the next hustle, but we never bought anything we could keep, never rented an apartment, and within a few weeks we'd be scrounging for down-low crack houses where we could lay up for the night in return for smoking their baby powder–laced rocks.

Occasionally, we'd take a vacation, head out of the city on a bus to a small town, where we could run a few cons. I had a tape recorder, just like the one Momma had given me when I was ten years old, and my favorite scam was making up commercials.

I'd stand on the sidewalk and say into my recorder: *Diane's Optical, for the best in class when it comes to glass. We've got sunglasses, fun glasses, contacts, and bifocals. If you've got eyes, we've got your prize. Take it from me, you'll see the Diane's difference.*

I'd walk into the business and introduce myself as a radio ad man, working for WXCK or one of the other major stations. Then I'd play them the recording. Their eyes always lit up when they heard my voice talking about their business. Their products never sounded so good.

I'd tell them, "We've got a special promotion right now. I can put this on the air five times a week, for five weeks, and all it will cost is two hundred dollars cash." They believed in me because I sounded like a radio man, and nobody with my voice could be wrong, right? I'd hit ten businesses in a day, collect a thousand dollars, and we'd be gone, back to Columbus on the last bus.

But I wasn't a radio man. I didn't even dream of being a radio man, not anymore. I was a criminal, living on a criminal drift, always on the move. Maybe it was shame, or maybe it was a poverty of the spirit, but I started to take pride in our life, in our ability to survive hand-to-mouth for years at a time. We weren't homeless, we were out-of-the-box entrepreneurs. Do you think Bonnie and Clyde had an address for mail? Do you think Jesse James went home to a mortgage at the end of the day? Do you think Robin Hood sat in the forest in some cabin, with a comfortable bed and a fire to keep him warm? No, he was hustling house to house, sleeping on the ground, hitting up friends, living off his wits. There was a romanticism to our life that I was spiritually bankrupt enough to believe, because we were living with no clock to punch and no bills to pay and no boss to bow down to but the pipe.

Every now and then, the law would catch us. I spent so much time in the city jail, I was like a regular performing act, The Radio Comedy Hour, playing to a packed house every six months. I had a nightly routine when the guards were checking the cells: *Can you turn a key from left to right? Can you say "Trays up," and "Roll 'em up?" Well then, you can be a Franklin County deputy. Call 1-800-DICKHEAD. That's 1-800-D-I-C-K-H-E-A-D.*

The other prisoners howled. They loved it. I was famous for that routine. Once when I was in court, a guy yelled at me, "Can you turn a key from right to left?" Man, we laughed over that one, like we'd shared a trip to Disney World or something.

Some of the guards liked it, too. They smiled, shook their heads, "All right, Radio," they said, "that's enough," but not mean, more like how Momma used to sigh when I practiced my radio voice too long. Sometimes, if there was a new guard, they'd say, "This is Radio, the guy we told you about. Radio, do your thing."

Can you turn a key from right to left . . .

Other guards weren't as pleased. They said, "I make twenty-eight dollars an hour, what are you making?" Or, "Yeah, well I go home at night, how about you?"

I loved doing my routine in the shower, because it was a big tiled room with amazing acoustics. I was always doing radio routines in the shower. I was in one night, soaping away, and started in like I always did with *Can you turn a key from right to left?* Listen to that echo. *Can you say, "Trays up," and "Roll 'em . . ."*

The water cut off.

"Hey, what's going on?"

I was covered in prison soap, which is lye, and if you don't get it off quick, it will burn your skin. So I started banging the wall, "Hey, the water's out. You got a water problem in here."

I heard a crackle and then a voice came over the intercom: "You should put in there 'we turn off showers, too.'"

So prison wasn't so bad. Since I was a cell-block celebrity, nobody hurt me. And crackheads don't have withdrawal like heroin addicts. Junkies got cramps so bad they couldn't eat or even stand up to grab their meal trays. Crackheads just got hungry. Very hungry. After a few sick days, I ate everything. I was so hungry, I ate my orange and carried the peel around with me. I put little peel pieces in my mouth and chewed them until they were gone. It wasn't nutritious, but it gave me the sensation of eating, and that was some sort of cure. It took all day, but I ate whole orange peels, nibble by nibble.

Of course, nothing changed. The minute I was out, I went looking for Kathy, and then for the crack house, and we went straight back to our old ways.

CHAPTER 17

f course, none of that's really the truth. The facts are true, absolutely, but the attitude? The pride? That's the old Ted Williams hustle. Trying to be positive, trying to hide the shame, telling stories about being a smart homeless man, a happy man, that I stopped believing long ago. Those first years, though I was still smiling, saying, *It's all right, people, Ted Williams is fine*, even though nobody was fooled. Because I was fooled. I believed it. To survive some days, I *had* to believe it, and lying to yourself is a hard habit to break.

But the truth is, there wasn't nothing glamorous about the life. Nothing fun about spending a few months every year in jail. Nothing positive about never taking showers, having terrible breath, rifling through rain-soaked clothes outside the Salvation Army drop box for something decent to wear. I was no fedora-clad gangster; I wasn't even a big-voiced pimp daddy; and I certainly wasn't giving to the poor. I was nothing more than a broken man desperately hustling for the next fix. Robbing banks? No, not me. I stole detergent, deodorant, toothpaste, and soap from drugstores. My big score was Oil of Olay face cream, because it was a small container, and it cost twenty-five dollars. You know how they lock up razors?

Bums like me caused that, because razors were good business. A Gillette Mach 3 was fifteen dollars (for a razor!), so I stole as many as I could hide. Then I bought something small, like a candy bar, and chatted up the clerk. There were times when the electronic monitor beeped on my way out, but the clerk waved me through because he thought there was no way a friendly, gregarious customer like me was robbing them blind.

I put the stolen items in paper bags and walked to a nightclub. Sometimes I sold the bag, sometimes I sold individual items, but I'd sell it all in five minutes. After a while, people started coming to me. "What you got, Radio?"

"I got cologne. Razors. Aftershave."

"Ah, you hooked me up with that last week."

"Well, what you need?"

I kept a client list in my head. I knew how long it had been since they bought, and what they were likely to need, so I tried to have that on hand. Sometimes, they made requests. These weren't criminals. These were regular working people. They knew where my stuff was coming from, it was obvious I wasn't a legit supplier, but they wanted a deal.

It got to the point where I'd walk down the street with a bag and people would pull their cars to the curb. "What you got today, Radio?"

"Just a Wendy's chili, man."

"Don't lie to me now."

"Nah, it's just my lunch."

"Well, look me up if you get some perfume. My girl's birthday is coming up."

Sometimes, I'd be standing on the corner with my bag and I'd see my kids walking on the other side of the street. Or even worse, I'd see them coming down my side of the street, then crossing over to avoid having to talk to me. My four daughters were teenagers by then, and the last thing they wanted was for their friends to know Daddy was a bum.

I'd call Momma, but it was the same. "Hi, Momma, it's me. It's Teddy."

"Are you working?"

"No, ma'am."

"Are you going to church?"

"No, ma'am."

She'd breathe—*hmmph*—and I could almost see the disapproval, even over the telephone line. We'd talk for a minute, I'd ask about my father, then we'd say good-bye, because there was nothing to say. I didn't lie to her anymore. I didn't use my radio voice—*Hey, Momma, this is Ted Williams, straight from Columbus O-hi-o*—to cover my shame or remind her of my potential. There was no money there, so I told the truth, and I never had any good truth to share.

Of course, she knew that already. She didn't need my calls to break her heart. She had relatives in Columbus rubbing her nose in it every time I appeared in *The Blotter*. She had my son Desmond's broken heart. She always told me how Desmond sounded when he said, "Mama Ted"—that's what my children called her—"I saw Daddy today. He didn't look so good."

Desmond was right. I didn't look good. Sometimes I was clean, with new clothes from the Salvation Army drop box, but even on good days my teeth were brown. My hair stood out in clumps from my head. My glasses were cracked. I was down to about 120 pounds, even though I'm six feet tall. It wasn't just crack killing my appetite. I'd eaten nothing but rice and fast food for years, as little as I needed to survive, and my stomach was torn up. I couldn't eat more than a few bites of solid food without getting nauseous.

Even worse, I carried myself like a bum. I carried myself like a man who didn't care about his appearance and didn't take care of himself, a man who was sick, or tired, or twenty years older than he should have been. I mean, I had pride, I didn't want to look like a bum, but I wasn't taking an honest look at myself. I lost myself in the pipe and said, *That's all right, Ted. You look bad today, but you'll look better tomorrow.* Then I'd see my children coming down the street, and I'd see their disgust, and I'd know I didn't look all right. I didn't look right at all.

Momma told me again and again, "You have a home, Teddy. You have a home right here, but you have to come alone."

But I was an addict. I didn't change. Even when my children held a mirror to my life, I didn't wash my hair. I shoplifted another store, took another hit, and the shame and guilt were gone, filling that emptiness under the crack smoke where self-respect used to be. And direction. And morals. And goals. I had been a Christian all my life, even when I was in the grip of my first addictions, but I had no God now. No love. I would look up to heaven and say, "God, help me get a hit today."

But when I had that hit, God was forgotten. I stopped looking to heaven and started looking into the pipe, into that flame.

That was all there was: the hustle, the pipe, the high. I can't tell you every day was the same, because I don't remember most of them. Kathy and I smoked and hustled, that was our entire lives. Sometimes we lay in a comfortable bed, sometimes we slept in jail, sometimes we passed out on the sidewalk in a crack coma, drooling down our shirts. I can't tell you what I did in 1998, but I can tell you that taken as a whole, 1999 was no different, and there was nothing to 1999 but drugs, drugs, drugs. After a while, it became routine. That's what you do, day after day, and nothing's going to change. Life will go on and on and on.

"You got a home, Teddy," my momma told me. "You can always come home." I could almost hear the unspoken part: *You're still my little boy.*

Then, in the winter of 2000, I called my momma, and instead of asking if I had a job, she said, "Your daddy died."

My father and I had had a broken relationship since 1978. We hadn't spoken in years, but there were still so many moments of happiness and love. I remember back in the hood, when they called us the Mod Squad: one white (me), one black (my daddy), and one blonde (my momma, with her blonde wig). I remember how we played catch, until he couldn't stand my girlie throws anymore. I remember Coney Island, not just the frog legs, but the way Daddy and I stood together looking at the ocean, talking about where it went. I remember our yearly trip to Rockaway Beach, when Daddy got us up at 4:30 in the morning to beat the traffic, and how the two of us went to the Caribbean on the spur of the moment one time, just took a cab to the airport and got on a plane. I remember the way he wore his hat, like he was out of some old jazz film.

I remember his pride when I was at the top of my life. I remember the way he smiled at that O'Jays concert, realizing his son was somebody at last. Long before I met Kathy, when I hated the very idea of white girls, I'd tell him, "Daddy, I dated a white girl!" just so he'd laugh and say, "I told you, son. I told you they were the best." The last thing I ever told him, in 1996, was about Kathy. He sounded excited. He wanted to meet the white girl his son finally brought home, even if his wife thought she was nothing but a junkie whore. But it never happened, we never got that chance.

Momma said, "I want you to stand by me, Teddy. I want you here for your father's funeral."

She was too heartbroken to make the arrangements, so she

handed the phone to my Aunt Lou. She and my uncle lived in Florida, but they were already in New York. Aunt Lou said, "Where are
you, Ted? I'm sending money for a round-trip plane ticket, so you
can be here tomorrow."

I went to Western Union, got the money, and took it straight to a
crack house. Kathy and I sat in that house and smoked rock after
rock. I couldn't stop. With each smoke, I felt my trip to New York
slipping away, and I felt guilty, *guilty*, until I finally started cursing Al
Williams, saying out loud in that filthy den, "He was no father to me."
Smoke. "He beat me up." *Smoke.* "He told me white people were better than blacks. He told me I was no good. He told me my dreams
were nothing." *Smoke.* "F*ck him, he wasn't even my real dad."

For two days straight I smoked my aunt and uncle's money. They
bought me clothes for the funeral, they set aside a room for me in
Brooklyn, New York, but on the day my father was laid to rest,
there was nothing in that room but an empty suit, hanging on the
back of a closet door.

I called my momma later that day, when I ran out of money. I
told her, "I lost the money, Momma. I need two hundred dollars
more to get home."

There was silence on the line for a long time. Then I heard a
voice so cold, it didn't even sound like Momma anymore. "How
dare you. How dare you call me for money, when you wouldn't even
stand by me at your father's funeral. Good-bye."

I put down the phone and fell on my knees. I bowed my head,
and for the first time since I'd been with Kathy, I prayed an honest
prayer. "Lord God," I prayed, "please don't take my momma. Please
let her live to see me off these streets.

"Please, God. Bring me home."

CHAPTER 18

Momma wouldn't speak to me after that. I tried to apologize, but for a year, all she said was, "Good-bye. Don't call here no more."

When she finally started talking, she said simply, "You could not even *stand* with me. You could not even be there when I lost my husband. Good-bye."

Sometimes her voice was cold. Sometimes it trembled. But it was always the same: You weren't here, Ted. You weren't here for me. She never said *your father*. She always said *my husband*. You could not even stand *with me* when my husband died.

When she said that, I felt it in my soul. I had disgraced the memory of my father when I skipped his funeral, I could see that, but I had also betrayed my momma. And I couldn't escape it. Momma had never done anything but love me. She had adopted me; she had gone to work in a school lunchroom for me; she had visited me in jail in North Carolina and sent me money and stood by me long after I had become nothing but a user of her love. I was her miracle child, and I had disappointed her beyond measure. I had given her nothing but pain.

When my friend Eric called his mother from the depths of his addiction, she told him, "You're killing me, son. I worry about you every day, and it's killing me." He took it to heart. He went to rehab, and although he relapsed back to the streets, he eventually pulled through. He got a real job, started visiting his mother in Dayton, called her three times every day.

My momma didn't have to tell me. She didn't have to say a word. I knew I was killing her. And what did I do? I put another rock on my pipe and I blasted away.

I wasn't sad. Not exactly. I was ashamed, and I was broken, and I hated myself . . . but I wasn't sad. That's a human emotion. For a crack junkie, there's only one happiness, and that's the rock. When you smoke, you feel joy. When you don't, you feel crushing despair.

I wanted to turn my life around. I prayed for my momma's health every day—or at least every day I spent time in my right mind. But she was so far from me, my children were so far from me, and my addiction was so close. It was my constant companion. There wasn't a moment on the street when I didn't think about crack. I had every reason to despair when I was sober, because I was a monster. I had hurt everyone that ever loved me. But in the years after my father died, most of my despair was simply this: I wanted to be high, and I wasn't, and it broke my heart.

Then I'd sit down with the pipe, and all would be forgotten. For me, that moment with the rock, when the hit became inevitable, was powerful. It was an almost religious experience. It was the moment in church, before the service, when you feel the presence of God. That sounds terrible, but it's true. The pipe was my salvation. The process of preparing a hit became its own high, something I hated to trade, because it was my communion. It takes a minute to pack a pipe, and I savored every second. I watched intently, especially if it was my first hit off a new rock, as my fingers worked the steps: stretching the chore, tearing, stuffing, breaking the rock, loading the piece, and finally firing up. *Acknowledge Him.* "Thank you, Jesus, for what I am about to receive." The joy in that moment, when the smoke hit my lungs. It felt like I was breathing the essence of life.

But it never lasted long. The hit was soon over, and then the rock was gone, and I was back on the street, hustling. It wasn't hunger anymore. I wasn't smoking to feed that emptiness inside me, that desire to be someone—to be loved and acknowledged and fulfilled. I was smoking to escape what I'd become. I kept doing what I was doing—stealing, smoking, living a dissolute life—*for eight more years* after my father died. For eight years, I buried my shame in the pipe.

And it took a toll. I developed a permanent sinus condition. My back ached, sometimes to the point of paralysis. My gums bled and my stomach clenched at the first swallow of food. I was constipated when I was smoking, and diarrhetic when I wasn't. I was forty-two years old, and needless to say, I wasn't living right. I wasn't drinking milk or taking vitamins. I wasn't visiting a dentist or eating vegetables. I never washed my hands. I never brushed my teeth. My glasses were scratched and twisted, but I never went to an eye doctor. My fingers had open cuts from tearing the metallic chore, but I never wore a bandage. I lived out in the rain in the summer, and in the winter, I spent nights in the snow. I got exercise because I walked all day and night in worn-out, ill-fitting shoes, which tore my feet to bits. I never sat down, except when I fell down, but I didn't rest. I slept in the bus station. Instead of buying motel rooms, I slept in their lobbies. Holiday Inn, Days Inn, Comfort Inn, if there's an "inn" in the name I crashed there. In a good week,

I got four nights of sleep and spent the other three nights awake, but more and more I passed out in crack houses and abandoned buildings, or even on a city sidewalk, high in the middle of the day.

Kathy's condition was worse because she was diabetic. There were times, many times, when I couldn't wake her. There were many times I thought she was gone, and I turned to my pipe wondering what to do with the corpse at my side. But the crack always brought her around. She could be out for a day, hardly breathing, but I'd light my twentieth hit and that crackling sound would sink into her brain somehow, and she'd open her bloodshot eyes, roll halfway toward me, and whisper, "Where's mine, you greedy SOB?"

We were stealing every few hours by then, a desperate sort of rush that took us all over Columbus, looking for new ground. We never used violence, never went into a building after hours, never broke into a car or threatened anyone. I've never carried a weapon, not even a knife. We were shoplifters and con artists, the sticky-fingered kind of criminals. We took food from gas stations to sell to dealers. We shoplifted from grocery stores. We stole clothes and books and cell phones and even car air fresheners, the pine tree kind you hang from your rearview mirror, anything we could trade for a buck.

One week, I noticed a fifteen-minute window at an electronics warehouse when no security guards were on duty, so I decided to pull my first big job. I hired a crackhead getaway driver for twenty dollars and then, when the time was right, grabbed two flat-screen televisions and ran for the door. I took about three steps and realized I was in such terrible physical shape I wasn't going to make it, I was going to have an aneurysm right there in the store. I staggered to the side, hit the edge of the door, stumbled onto the sidewalk, and turned to face my two pursuers (and catch my breath).

They pulled up short, the first guy stopping so fast the second one almost knocked him down, and at the time I thought it was my golden voice shouting (between gulping breaths), "Don't . . . try it" that stopped them. Now I realize that I looked so dirty, deranged and, well . . . "street" that they were probably afraid of what I might do next.

A disaster, that's what it was. The crackhead could barely drive. My shoulder felt ripped out of its socket. I wasn't cut out for pawning big-ticket items. I was willing to accept whatever lowball amount the fence was offering, because in ten minutes that money would turn into crack.

Kathy drove the bargains. She never settled for less than half the real value, even if we had to drive to three fences or hold on to the merchandise for a few days. "I work too hard," she always said. "I work too hard to get taken." She didn't mean the specific job. She meant everything she did to survive.

I hated her for that: for her love of money, for her greed for crack, for her taking her pain and heartbreak and wearing it like a suit of armor against the world. And yet, that hardness was the very thing that kept us alive, because Kathy was always pushing forward, always figuring out a way to make another score. It didn't matter that her looks had eroded over the years into stringy hair, messed up teeth, and sunken cheeks. It didn't matter that there were many times when I was ashamed to be with her, she looked so bad. Kathy could talk. She could make certain men desire her, the ones who wanted a woman to tell them what to do. She took the free meals and showers she'd been getting for years, and she pushed them into longer and longer stays, more and more gifts, by the pure force of her will.

She was a con artist. She figured out what men wanted, and she relentlessly pushed the idea on them—not the act, but the idea—until she hooked them. Companionship. Excitement. Even the promise of sex. There were a lot of lonely men, and they took Kathy on vacations, to fancy dinners, even to their homes in neighboring states.

She'd be gone for weeks without a word, and there were a few times, I know, when she thought about staying away for good. Why wouldn't she? These men offered more than Ted Williams could provide—like food, a clean toilet, a safe place to lay her head. By all rights, she should have gone away with them. A lot of these guys had money. They gave her everything she wanted and more.

She always called me in the end, though, and I'd travel up to live with her man, using our old brother-sister routine. These were usually older men with problems, alcoholism or maybe drugs. She treated them well, at least for a time. I witnessed the happiness she gave them. But it always ended badly for those men because the two of us couldn't stay, and we always cleaned them out before moving on.

One man gave her a checkbook, so we wrote ten thousand dollars to cash, then passed the checks through a check cashing business. The bank called several times to check the payments, but Kathy had given them my cell phone number. I always told them to put the payment through.

A rich businessman gave Kathy her own credit card. We ran up fifteen thousand dollars in charges before we overdrew the account.

A trick had a collection of sports memorabilia. He loved it. He'd been collecting all his life. We stole it. Another had a shrine to his dead mother in his living room. We stole that, too.

One gentleman took us in for three or four months, a good guy with a big drinking problem. He had a nice house with a pool, and he didn't mind buying things for his lover and her brother. He never suspected evil intentions, and even though I'm sure he noticed a few things missing, he never questioned me about them. He was in love with Kathy—crazy, head over heels in love. He knew she was a prostitute, he knew she smoked drugs, but he thought he could save her. Seriously, he thought he could take my girl off the street and make her the princess she was always meant to be.

Eventually, it got to me. I couldn't take being on the outside of Kathy's life, even with the big house . . . the nice bed . . . the endless piña coladas by the pool. I couldn't stand the way that man put his arm around her, the way he smiled in her presence, and the way she put her head on his shoulder. So I told him. I said, "Listen up, fool. She's not my sister. She's my girl, and she's been f*cking me behind your back the whole time."

Then I walked straight out the door, down to the station, and took the next bus to Columbus. I didn't know what was going to happen. I thought maybe that was the end. But two days later, Kathy found me on the street, and we went right back to the crack house and the raggedy end of skid row, right back to doing what we do.

Kathy

I thank Julia Roberts. In my forties, I was able to move from tricks in motel rooms to nice houses in the suburbs. I was able to trade up from sex-hounds and victimizers to men who didn't want me to have sex and leave, and who often didn't want me to have sex at all, and it was partially because of her. These men saw something in me: not a human being, but a project. They said they loved me, but what they really loved was the idea of me. Julia Roberts made that happen. She made the fantasy of turning a prostitute, of saving her and making her your respectable girlfriend, or even your wife, seem like a legitimate goal. Twenty years later, johns were still dreaming about *Pretty Woman*, the ultimate hooker advertisement.

It never worked like that, though. Because I was an addict. Because I wasn't interested in them, at least not as human beings. I wanted their money, not their time, their attention, or their so-called affection. Most of these guys weren't beaters or cheaters, like the street johns. They weren't out paying for sex with wedding rings on. But they weren't innocent either. They weren't picking me up on a dating service.

"Another victim."

That's what I told Ted every time I walked out to solicit, whether it was a quick twenty or a long-term shakedown. Someone was going to be victimized. That was the nature of the business. I've had a body built for sex since a very young age, so for a long time that victim was me. Raped at twelve. Hit on by my father's friends at fifteen. I looked like I wanted it, I guess. But I didn't. I wanted to screw those guys, but not the way they thought. The 98 percent rule. "Another victim." They meant the same thing. Ninety-eight percent of the time, I was going to win.

I just needed the right kind of man. Someone with a habit. A timid personality. A non-sexual emptiness. Someone with a home, preferably in another city or distant suburb. Someone, ideally, with retirement or disability payments, because they received monthly checks. I could have lived well. I was older, but I was wise; and I was meeting guys with mega money in those later years. One man took me on vacation to Florida. Another gave me a ten-thousand-dollar checking account. I lived with a lonely businessman in a gorgeous house for half a year. He was generous and kind. He gave me a swimming pool, a car, a stable life, everything. But I couldn't leave Ted.

Ben, on the other hand . . . Ben was trouble. I knew that right away, but he was the one I couldn't resist. He was like my brother's bad friends, the ones I had always thrown away my sanity for. He was young and handsome, with a pair of boots, a pickup truck, and an obvious dark side.

He also had money. He had thrown himself out a window for the insurance settlement, and in addition to a large lump sum, he was getting a nice check a couple times a year. He spent most of that money on drugs—OxyContin, heroin, the real damaging stuff. He was the worst kind of addict, really. He didn't do anything but drugs.

He seemed like the perfect mark.

And, I admit, he seemed like a good time.

He lived in a small town outside Columbus, so I moved there. It wasn't a good life. Ben was an unstable guy. He was always on edge because he shot up every day. He'd get high and scream at me, accuse me of stealing. Which I wasn't, not this time, because Ben scared me. He beat people up for looking at me wrong, or for no reason at all. He was more vicious, and less rational, than anyone I'd ever been around.

I ended the relationship a few times, but he always bought me something to bring me back. He bought me jewelry. He bought me a fancy pedigreed dog. He bought me a truck—because he had lost his license and had so many felony driving charges, he could never get it back. Eventually, he took me on vacation to New Mexico.

It turned out to be a drug deal. He bought fifty pounds of marijuana, stashed it in my suitcase, *which had my name right on the tag*, and forced me to carry it back to Ohio on a bus.

Within weeks, forty pounds had been stolen. He accused me. I hadn't stolen it. He was a blackout drug addict, and any number of people could have taken it. But he focused on me. He beat me. He threatened to kill me if I left without paying him back. He had a contract out on Ted, he told me. All he had to do was say the word. And that depended on me.

One day, I talked back. The next day, Ted was dead. Ben didn't tell me the details, just that he'd been shot. I believed him. Ben knew people. He had money. He had a dark anger and no morals, absolutely none. Killing Ted would have been easy for him.

It would have been easy for him to kill me, too.

So I stuck. For a month, I stayed with him in utter terror. Even crack couldn't save me. So when he passed out one night, I took five hundred dollars from his wallet—leaving five hundred for him—and drove his truck to Columbus. I was so relieved when I found Ted, so relieved. It may sound corny, but everything I did, *everything*, I did for Ted. For us. I never for a second imagined my life without him.

Two days later, Ben called me. He seemed almost relieved, like our mutual months of torment were over. Like holding me prisoner so long had worn him down. I didn't trust him, but I decided to meet him. I had to give him his truck, or I knew I'd never be rid of him. So I got together five hundred dollars to pay him back, and I drove to a motel. I knocked at the door. He said, "Come in." I stepped inside. I felt the explosion, and the world staggered. I saw Ben rear back, something in his hand, and I felt the explosion again and again until, in abject terror, I blacked out on the floor.

I woke up tied to the bed. The pain was so intense, I couldn't open my mouth. It felt like everything inside my head was broken. I found out later I had cracked ribs and a broken sternum. But I couldn't feel it, not for days, because I couldn't get past the pain in my head. It was so crippling I couldn't move. I couldn't focus. I couldn't formulate thoughts. All I could comprehend was Ben pacing, then standing over me, then bending toward me with a needle.

It turned out Ben had been shooting up cocaine and OxyContin since I left him, working himself into a black rage. When I walked in the door, he hit me across the head with a wooden board he'd pried off the motel bed. I'm not sure what happened, exactly, but the first shot might have cracked my skull. It definitely broke teeth. I could feel the shards with my tongue.

Now Ben didn't know what to do. He couldn't let me go. If anyone saw me in that state, he'd be tried for attempted murder. So he shot me with heroin—a drug I'd never used and haven't since—and kept me tied to the bed.

For a month.

And for a month, nobody called. Nobody came looking for me. My family was used to long silences. Ted thought I was in a nice house somewhere. I didn't have anybody else. When my head cleared, that thought tormented me. Nobody was coming. Nobody cared. Only Ben, my worst nightmare, knew where I was.

He almost killed me. Every day, I thought he was going to. It was his easiest way out. But God was watching. That's how I look at it now. God wouldn't let me go. Not that way. He wouldn't let me be a small headline on the last page of a local newspaper: Crack Whore Beaten to Death. Even my wasted life was worth more. So He saved me. At my worst moment, God saw me through. He sent me home.

I never went to a hospital. I didn't even visit the free clinic. I returned to Columbus and went straight back to my old life. Back to the street. Back to my drug of choice.

Back to Ted.

CHAPTER 19

There was no joy in the life we were living, no joy at all. Our lives were sadness and fear, for the most part, along with depression, desperation, and the growing sense that our habits were catching up with us. My teeth ached, my stomach burned, my feet were covered with sores. For years, Kathy had used the earpieces of my glasses to push hot chore through the pipe, until both earpieces finally melted off. So I had no glasses. I had to squint to see two feet in front of me, but that wasn't so bad, I guess, because there was nothing much to see anyway.

We were dregs, that's what it felt like. By the late 2000s, the world had moved on from crack, and we were the wounded left behind. There was still a crack world, a big one, don't get me wrong, but it had gone underground. "Crack is whack," that's what the hip-hop generation said. They may have started out slinging to fools like me, but most never used. They saw crack steal my generation's soul, and most of them left it alone. A youngblood said to me once, "You got talent, man, what you doing on the street?"

His friend put his fingers to his lips, imitating the pipe. "Brother smokes."

The youngblood nodded. Nothing else needed to be said. The sentence was self-explanatory. Talent's nothing to crack. Crack lays everybody low.

And eventually, it lays you flat, because a body can take only so much. A longtime smoking buddy passed out in an alley and never woke up. Another tried to administer insulin for his diabetes while high and went into a coma. He died the next day. A dozen more simply disappeared. A friend was decapitated thirty minutes after our last conversation when she slammed a rental truck into a telephone poll. Rumor said they had to pry the crack pipe out of her dead hand, because she was lighting a hit when she lost control.

We were up at Mom's, a crack den on the east end, where an addicted old granny ("Mom") let dealers sell out of her house in exchange for rocks. Kathy was lighting a rock in the back room when the pipe broke in her hand. She looked down in shock, half blasted, and noticed she was gushing blood. A girl went to help her wash up, and Kathy was halfway through cleaning herself when she looked over and saw the girl smoking her broken pipe. It was full of Kathy's blood, and the end was jagged and sharp, but there was a little rock in there somewhere, and the girl was boiling blood, trying to catch smoke. I doubt she's alive today.

Because addiction is a sickness. It's a creeping lack of control. I had a long-standing rule never to buy from a baller, a street addict who buys an eight ball, smokes half, and sells the rest to desperate losers for extra cash. But my standards slid along with my health, and it was late one night, and I was hungry. The baller on the corner took my money, looked over his shoulder, and as he dropped the rock into my hand he whispered, "It's the cops, yo. Beat it."

He took off running one way, I ran the other, and when I finally looked into my hand I was holding a piece of Lemonhead candy.

Man, I cursed myself then, because I'd always been the bag man, even when I was a kid I ran the cigarettes for the old folks in the building, and after all those years, I couldn't believe I'd been scammed. It was my last dollar, too, so I put that Lemonhead in my pipe and smoked it.

"Lord, please," I prayed.

But that didn't work. You can't smoke a Lemonhead. It will burn, I can tell you that from experience, but you can't get high off sugar and dye.

You've got to hit bottom, right? That's what everybody says. But where was the bottom when the bottom was your life? Was it when I tried to smoke a Lemonhead? Or when I started eating food out of Dumpsters? I took a certain pride in that, though. "Vietnam m*therf*cker," I always said before taking a bite of discarded rubbish, because eating like that made me think of the American soldiers in Vietnam, out surviving in the bush on nothing but bugs.

Was it when I visited my daughter Julia and ate all her baby's food? There must have been fifteen jars, and I sat down and ate them one after the other. Julia was a single mother, she was struggling, but I couldn't stop. When I saw the look on her face, I knew I'd done wrong. I looked down at her nine-month-old baby, and I realized I'd taken food out of my own grandson's mouth.

I told Momma I was coming home, and she said, "Don't do it. It's not going to work. There's no home for you here." Was that the bottom?

I begged, "Please, Momma. I want to see where Daddy's buried."

"Buried! Your father's not buried, fool. He was cremated. He's right here on my living room shelf."

One day, in the middle of a fight, I broke Kathy's arm in three places. I barely touched her, but her bones snapped. We wrapped her arm in a dirty towel and—where do you think we went?—to

Mom's crack house for a blast. The police raided the place the next morning. They usually roughed us up during a raid, but Kathy got lucky; she was grabbed by a female cop, and I can still hear her begging, "Please. I'm hurt. Please take me to a hospital."

They booked her, then sent her to County, where a doctor set her arm and said, "Those toes need to come off."

Kathy looked down. The three smallest toes on her left foot were black. Diabetes, no circulation. She was living so hard, she had no idea her body was dying. She begged them not to take her foot, so they delayed the surgery for a week. The forced rest and three square meals in prison worked. The blood came back. The flesh lived. Jail food saved Kathy's foot.

But even that wasn't rock bottom. Not to me anyway. When I think of rock bottom, I think of the colonel. He was a retired military officer, crack addicted and bisexual, and one of Kathy's gay friends found him in a chat room. By the time I arrived on the scene, Kathy and her friend had bilked him of about fifteen thousand dollars, mostly by writing checks out of his bank account. The colonel didn't seem to care, or so I told myself. He had property and investments but no children, so it wasn't anything to him.

We really hit it off, the colonel and me. We had Kathy and the armed forces in common, and of course crack cocaine. We chatted all the time, man-to-man, and Kathy used our relationship to string him along for a few more months, take him for another ten thousand dollars or so, mostly through late-night withdrawals from ATM machines.

Eventually, the three of us ended up in a motel, smoking crack. Even by our standards, it was a raggedy motel, but the colonel was buying, so we were smoking, hit after hit, day after day. The old man was a perpetual money and drug machine; everybody was happy because everybody was high—until the colonel started wanting to get a little friendlier with me.

It started out as nothing, a passing thought between hits, until Kathy got hold of it and negotiated the colonel up to a thousand dollars, all while I'm sitting there with the pipe to my mouth, thinking, *Hell no. Oh, hell no.*

Then the offer was on the table, and it was serious. It was pretty clear the party was going to end if I didn't go along.

So I started considering the idea, and the longer it hung in the air, mixing with that beautiful crack smoke, the more possible it seemed, until I'd almost made up my mind to do it, to have gay sex with the colonel for money. Then I looked over at him lounging on a chair, his lips around the pipe, his beaten face and still-muscled arms reflected in the lighter's flame, and I said, "I can't do it."

Kathy sprang up.

"I'm not going to do it, Kathy."

She stopped. She started to say something. But she must have seen the determination in my eyes, she must have known that was my final answer, because instead of speaking, she went wild.

She lunged at me. "You son of a bitch." She swung her fist at my head, then plowed into me, knocking me to the floor. We fought like dogs, scratching and clawing, until I finally busted out of the motel room door. I was running down the block, no shoes, broken glass and needles everywhere. Kathy was ten steps behind me, her shirt ripped, throwing shoes and rocks and beer cans at me, yelling, "You son of a bitch, you lousy son of a bitch, you could have made us a thousand dollars—*a thousand dollars!*—and all you had to do was let him suck your dick."

Rock bottom. That's rock bottom, right there. The place from which you can only go up . . . or check out.

Kathy

When I met John a few weeks after Ben let me go, my mind still wasn't right. I was suffering terrible headaches. I was dizzy. I was seeing shadows. There were flashes behind my eyes. And I was terrified. Scared of the johns, scared of the smokers in the crack houses, absolutely terrified Ben was coming after me. Even Ted didn't make me feel safe anymore.

So when John said he lived a few hundred miles away, I agreed to move there with him. I mean, it felt like God had set it up. I had been so deep in the rabbit hole it had scared even me. Now I had the opportunity to get away. I lived with John for a long time—it might have been six months or maybe a year. I liked him, he was a good guy. I missed Ted, my life felt unreal without him, but I was scared of going back. Scared because of Ben. Ted says, "You left me." He still says that to me. "You left me for a year." But it's not true. I never left him, not in my heart.

I left crack, though. For months and months, I was clean. I smoked a little pot, and John was an alcoholic, but we lived, basically, a normal life. We had a church. A neighborhood. A nice house and new car, with insurance paid six months in advance.

Then we got into a fight. I don't even know what it was about. My niece was being confirmed into the Catholic Church, and we were going to Columbus to celebrate with my sisters. Then suddenly, out of nowhere, things turned ugly. I'll never forget how John threw my bags in the trunk, slammed it shut, and said, "Go to Columbus. We'll see in a few days if this is going to work out."

"Please," I said. "Please."

"Go," he said, turning his back on me.

It was February. It was snowing. I drove around in circles for an hour, calling John again and again, pleading to stay. I knew what was going to happen if I went back to Columbus alone.

"Go," he said. "I want you to see your family."

Halfway to Columbus, I convinced myself John wasn't taking me back. I had two thousand dollars in my bank account and the new car. I figured that's what he was giving me to go away.

I went to my niece's confirmation. Then I went to dinner with my sisters, the first meal I'd had with them in ten years. It was beautiful. The whole day was beautiful. It was the only time, I think, between my brother's death in 1996 and 2010, where I felt like a member of the family. Like I was a person they could love.

I should have gone home with one of my sisters. I should have driven back to John and asked for a second chance. At the very least, I should have gotten a motel room. But I didn't. I kept driving around, thinking about Ted, delaying. Eventually, my thoughts turned to a gay friend who lived in the Bottoms, one of the city's worst neighborhoods.

In the end, I broke down. I drove to the Bottoms. I pulled up to my friend's building and sat for twenty minutes in my car. Then I went inside, peeling off a twenty-dollar bill, and said, "How about we share a rock?"

I took a hit—one hit—and it almost killed me. My eyes popped. My throat burned. I started vomiting and then, suddenly, I was on the floor, crying, because the crack was killing me. I could feel it. It was killing me. And I wanted to go home.

I called my sister Chris, who lived in the suburbs. At dinner, I had talked about living with her for a while, until I got back on my feet. But that was hours before.

"Chris, I need to get to your house. How do I get to your house?"

Silence. Long silence. "Have you been smoking?"

"No. I'm clean, Chris. I want to come home."

She didn't believe me. She thought I was high, and she didn't want anything to do with me. I started crying. Really crying, something I never did. I saw my life in that moment. I was weak. Evil. Cursed. If Chris didn't bring me home, I'd lose my car. I'd lose my bank account. I'd be back on the street, a hopeless addict. I didn't want that. I never wanted that. But I couldn't walk away on my own.

"I only had one hit, Chris. But I didn't like it. I don't want it anymore." I was desperate. So desperate. "I don't want it, Chris. I hate it. Please bring me home."

"No."

I begged. I begged like I never had before, with my whole heart. She was adamant. She had young kids. I was high. I hadn't changed. She couldn't risk a drug addict in her home.

I hung up the phone in despair. Total despair. I fell back on the couch, fully aware that my life was over. I was going to die on the street in my addiction. I was going to die a whore. I couldn't fight it anymore. It was what I deserved.

But I didn't want to die alone. That was the one thing left to me: my soul mate. My Ted. I wanted to die, if I must, with the man I loved.

CHAPTER 20

was living in the woods behind a Meijer's grocery store. It may
have been 2008, although I can't be entirely sure. Kathy was in
jail or away with a client, so I was lying low. There was maybe
half a mile of woods, and I was far enough back from the road that
no one could see me lighting up. And by no one, I don't mean cops
and ordinary people, I mean other homeless. They were in the
woods, too. I could see their lighters when I walked at night. I
feared the homeless worse than the cops, because nobody living
wild wants strangers in their stuff. A homeless person will guard
his squat like it's the White House.

It wasn't a bad lay-up. I had a mattress, a blanket, a bucket for
slops. I stumbled on a box of children's raincoats in an alley, so I
went Vietnam m*therf*cker and taped them together to form a
mostly watertight cover. I had a crack house nearby, and when I
wasn't high, I could wallow alone in my depression and addiction,
which by that time I preferred to company anyway. I had been muttering to God since the colonel, been trying to curb some bad habits, like cursing, but for all my half-baked attempts to raise myself

from the bottom, it was nothing but the same mindless existence that had gone on and on for years.

Then, one day, I was sitting on a crate, minding my own business, when I heard clomping in the woods. I thought, *Deer!*—and fear jumped into my heart. But when I looked through the underbrush, I didn't see deer. I saw a big black man in a three-button suit, picking his way up my hill. He was crushing garbage under his Italian shoes and stopping every few steps to knock dirt off the soles. By the time he reached the patch of ground I called home, he had mud splattered to his knees.

"How you doing, Ted?" he said, checking out my spread. "You ready for some work?"

"Yes, sir."

That man was Al Battle, my only remaining friend from the radio game. Al was a local concert promoter, and back in the early 1990s, during my first recovery, he often hired me to record his radio commercials. He didn't forget me or my voice after I disappeared into the streets in 1996. Every few months, I'd hear from a homeless brother, "That well-dressed black man looking for you again, Radio. Said to be down on the corner tomorrow morning."

Or I'd be minding my own business, selling stolen toiletries, and Al would roll up in his SUV, roll down his window, and say, "How you been, brother? You taking care of yourself?"

Al had his own recovery story, like so many others. His uncle Karl Russell was one of the lead singers for the Hues Corporation, a band that hit it big in 1974 with "Rock the Boat" (*"Rock the boat, don't rock the boat baby, tip the boat, don't tip the boat over"*). Russell invited Al, a promising musician, to come out to California and play bass for the band. Straight from the hood to Hollywood, as Al put it, and all within a week of graduating from high school.

The next years were tiptop: television appearances, contracts, money. Al was riding the wave of fame, touring the country, playing concerts while being wined and dined. At nineteen, he went to a party at RCA and hung out with Billy Preston, Ike Turner, Richard Jones, and T. Rex. Someone laid some lines on a table and said, "Try that, youngblood from Ohio." Strong cocaine, the pure stuff. It hit like a rocket, and it made Al want to pick up his bass and play.

Pretty soon, Al was convinced he couldn't play without coke, couldn't make his music without the drug. He was using every day, every time he played, and then the gigs died down, the band broke up, and he didn't have music anymore. But he still had his habit. By the early 1980s, he was out of the music industry and dead broke, living for the next high. Then one evening, he found himself fighting a bum over a refrigerator box on L.A.'s skid row.

He said to himself, *You're Al Battle. Al Battle doesn't fight for refrigerator boxes.*

He cleaned up, took a job as an eleventh-grade graphic arts teacher, got his life back together. During the second year, he dated a fellow teacher. They were going to get an apartment together, but instead of paying the deposit he took the rent money and blew it on drugs. A few months later, he was out of work again, sitting in front of Grauman's Chinese Theatre with nothing but an Afro comb, a toothbrush, and his snorting tools. He was sick of his life, sick of spiraling, because everything he'd loved was gone and all he had left was powder. So he got on his knees, right on Hollywood Boulevard, and prayed.

"God, if you don't take this affliction from me today, I'm going to kill myself." He didn't mean suicide. He meant he was going to snort himself into oblivion.

The answer came back, *Go to the employment office.*

He thought, *I'm not looking for a job, Lord. I'm looking for a cure.*

Go to the employment office.

He went. He took the bus across town, registered for a counselor, turned around, and saw his high school girlfriend sitting across the room. She said, "Al Battle?"

"Yeah, Brenda, it's me."

They started dating. Al did a thirty-day program, did Al-Anon, and got a job cutting the cloth for women's panties on the conveyor belt at the Olga factory in L.A.

"I was fighting," Al told me. "I was fighting to get clean. But I wasn't ready yet, deep inside. I just wanted to make sense out of the chaos I'd been living, and when I did, I thought I could use. I saw other people using on the weekends, and their lives weren't messed up, and I thought I could do that, too. I just disregarded everything I had learned."

One evening, he went out for a bucket of chicken. He didn't come back for thirty days. He had the rent money in his pocket, so he figured he could score a big bag of coke, flip most of it for profit, and keep a little taste for himself. But each time he flipped, he bought again, and each time he bought, his taste got bigger, until there wasn't anything left to snort or sell. By the time he made it home, he was broke—with no fried chicken.

His girlfriend opened the door and said, "Oh, Al. Oh, Al, are you all right?"

He hadn't showered in a month, he'd been living on the street, but she rushed right out and hugged him. "Come in, baby. Come in. Are you hungry? Can I get you a shower?"

He broke down. He fell to his knees and starting crying, right in the front room, because her kindness broke his heart. She didn't know he had a drug problem, she found out he was using only when he disappeared, but she didn't hold nothing against him. She stood by him. She took him in her arms, put him in the bathtub, and all he could say was, "I used to be somebody. I used to be somebody."

They moved back to Columbus. They got married. Al went to the treatment center at Mercy Hospital, and when he came out in 1985, they started a family, two beautiful children, and he's been clean ever since. He started a business promoting concerts, mostly bands but some comedy acts, too, and that's when I met him for the first time, in the early 1990s, during my first stretch on the streets.

Al didn't mind my low condition. In fact, he wanted to help. When I was the Relapse King from 1993 to 1996, Al gave me voice-over work and took me to Narcotics Anonymous meetings. He gave me money when I asked, even though he knew I was using it for drugs, because he was a former addict. He understood I was going to get mine somehow, and that to have a chance to change my life, he had to stay in my life.

I lost track of him after my world collapsed in 1996, except when he hunted me down. Sometimes, when he found me, I was in pretty good shape. We'd laugh and joke like old times.

But as the years went by, we saw each other less, and when he came around then, more often than not I was living low. That day in the woods, I remember, I was strung out bad. I thought I was keeping it tight, but as soon as I climbed in Al's car, I knew something was wrong. I could smell it. I was as foul as the rotgut junkies I used to shake my head at down at Open Shelter. Then it hit me for the first time: I *was* one of those rotgut junkies.

We rode in silence for a while, avoiding the subject, and then we both started laughing, more out of nervousness than anything else. "Ted, you reek, man," Al said.

"I know, I know, Al. I'm sorry."

"I'm going to get you a shower." We drove in silence a little while longer. "I'm going to get this car fumigated, too."

I took the shower, ate as much as I could on my rotten stomach, and went up to the studio to record my commercials. I admit, I always stole a few things on my way into and out of the recording session, because that was part of who I was. I couldn't stop myself. I figured out later Al would clear the studio as much as possible before I arrived, and I suppose he just paid for what I took. He was getting a nice deal off me anyway, and those commercials sounded good. I heard them once in a while, when I passed a radio, and they lit me up.

That's me, I'd think. *Radio on the radio. I still got it.*

After the session, Al asked me to stay at one of his houses. He was working a few properties, rented them cheap to recovering addicts or ex-cons, offering responsibility and an address while they turned their lives around. "I'll let you stay free," Al told me, "if you paint a room."

"Nah," I said, "that's nice of you, Al, but I don't want to stay out there."

I wasn't in the right frame of mind. I didn't see an opportunity. I saw trouble. I would have to take care of Al's house, make sure it was clean, make sure nothing got broke. I was going to smoke in that house, because I was an addict, and while that wasn't against Al's rules, it presented all kinds of problems. I'd be in a new area, so I'd have to find a new place to cop. And if that proved difficult, which it probably would, I'd have to resist the temptation to call one of my old dealers, because they'd come out to the house and realize it was a safe spot, and pretty soon, if I wasn't careful, there'd be a crack house running out of Al's generosity. The end result, without a doubt, would be alienating Al and losing my last link to radio.

And besides, I didn't like leaving my stuff in the woods. The thought of some crackhead rifling my possessions, touching my blanket and sleeping on my mattress, was enough for me to say, "Thanks, Al, but I can't. Not this time."

And maybe that's the surest sign I was truly homeless after all: I felt more comfortable sleeping in the woods under a raincoat-taped-together tent than I did in a real bed in a real house.

But I wasn't finished yet. I wasn't hopeless, which to me defines true homelessness: a hopeless state of mind. When you have no hope of a way out, because you have given up on yourself completely, you are truly a homeless man. But even on my darkest day, Al reminded me, I had my voice.

Day after day, year after year, I had sucked crack smoke, drug impurities and lighter fluid over my vocal cords. When I didn't have a lighter, I lit a kerosene-soaked rag and inhaled straight off the flame. Sometimes, when Kathy and I laid up in recently abandoned houses, we'd light a pipe off the gas stove. It was common to blacken the ceiling of those abandominiums, as we called our long-term indoor lay-ups, with our fire and smoke.

But even after all that smoke, my voice survived. Even after the abuse, it still had a deep honey sound like my hero Hank Spann. It still had resonance, with a thick timbre behind. It still moved Al Battle to hire me, and it moved radio listeners to attend his shows. And because of that, I had hope. I sat up in my raincoat tent that night, with my crack pipe, and I swore to myself I'd try again. *One more run at sobriety, Ted. One more run.* I looked at that litter-strewn patch of woods, and my homeless-man rags, and thought, *You can make it, Ted. There is still a way.*

And that's why the most honest prayer of my life was probably the one I prayed that night. I took the pipe in my hand, raised it to my lips, and said, "I know I don't have a right, Lord. I know I'm doing wrong. But please, Lord . . . please spare my golden voice."

CHAPTER 21

A year later, in 2009, Kathy and I were laid up in the entryway of an abandoned Mexican restaurant, one of our best living arrangements. A big awning, bordered by the building on one side and a half-wall with bushes on the other, sheltered us from the weather. We had a real mattress (courtesy of a motel Dumpster) and an endless supply of clean sheets, courtesy of a nearby motel's maid cart. We had motel bottles of soap and shampoo, buckets for water and waste, two wooden crates for night tables, even an old bench for sitting or using as a table. We rigged a clothesline so Kathy could dry her two outfits after scrubbing them in the water bucket, and we even had umbrellas to keep out spring's driving rains. Al Battle came by one day to pick me up for a recording session, and even he used our bathroom facilities.

"That's not bad, Ted," he said, coming out from behind our privacy sheet. "That's a nice setup." Can you imagine that, a straight-living man complimenting a street person's bathroom?

Even better, our camp was private. The restaurant was at the end of an access road off a highway exit, so we were hidden from the street. The neighborhood was suburban, so there were fewer street people and hasslers, but there was access to dope in the apartments half a block away. Kathy could pick up johns in the three nearby motels, which looked like regular highway-exit businesses (and probably were, for all I know), but were full of traveling salesmen and hookers. The police drove by our squat every now and then, but the entry road and parking lot were long and open, so we'd see them coming and hide our pipes in the bushes, because by then the War on Drugs had made owning a crack pipe a crime.

The cops would pull up, roll down their window, and say, "That you in there, Radio?"

I'd hop out from behind the bushes, "Yes, sir. It's me."

"All right, Radio, take care of yourself. Don't cause any trouble."

It was an ideal spot, really, a great place to live. It gave me a quiet space in the world, where I could contemplate my life. For months, maybe even since that night in the woods, I'd had two words rattling around in my head: *Acknowledge Him.* They were part of Proverbs 5–6, a Bible verse that meant a lot to me during my recovery in 1996. Every time I sat down to eat, I thought of those words, *Acknowledge Him,* and I bent my head in prayer. Even if the food came from a Dumpster, I told Kathy, "We have to acknowledge God," and we both folded our hands to pray.

We had a scam we'd been using to get free meals for years. I'd call a restaurant and use the old-Jewish-guy voice from my Southeast Seafood commercial. "Hi, excuse me, sir. I'm sorry to call, but I ate in your restaurant last week and, I hate to complain, but the food was not good. My wife, she had the soup, and there was something wrong, it tasted terrible. She's been sick over it for a week. What? A free meal? Well, that's nice of you, thank you, but I'm old, my wife is sick, can my daughter come down and pick it up? Great. Thank you, sir. I'll send her down. Her name is Kathy."

We'd sit in a stairwell with our stolen meal and *Acknowledge Him.*

In the crack house, holding the lighter above the pipe, I'd think of those two words and say, "Thank you, God, for what I am about to receive."

The other addicts hated that. They'd yell, "Shut up, man. There ain't no God in a crack house."

"Oh, He's here," I'd say, blowing a cloud of smoke. "He's watching over us right now."

It was wrong, I know, to call out to God like that. It was wrong to think the Lord was condoning my sins. But the words helped. They reminded me to look beyond my own needs. Acknowledging God made me realize He was out there, and He was watching. It gave me a reason to do right—or at least to try. I didn't worry too much about my failings. *Progress not perfection*, that's what recovery taught me. Be mindful. Put in the effort. Make progress every day.

Acknowledge Him in ALL your ways, that's how the Bible put it. God cared about everything, in other words, and if that was true, then changing small things mattered, right? I couldn't cold-turkey my crack addiction or stop the illegal means of supporting myself. The life had me too much in its grip. But I could watch my words, and that progress might push me down the path.

So I stopped cursing, along with my prayers. I stopped using n*gger as a slur, and I tried to stop Kathy from using it, because that was another bad habit I'd given her. I stopped taking the Lord's name in vain, stopped saying GD my pipe, GD my aching back, GD the Wendy's hamburger I could barely keep down.

I know it doesn't seem like much, compared to my other sins, but the effort mattered to me, because day after day, if I caught myself cursing, I stopped. I said, "Sorry, Lord."

And when I said "sorry," I thought of His presence. And I felt so inspired by His presence that eventually I started talking to Him. Not just rambling. Not just praying and asking, but talking . . . about my day, my decisions, the things I'd done. The life was a grind, but our restaurant squat give me the space to think about my sins. Sometimes, I thought I was crazy, a homeless man on a wooden crate outside an abandoned restaurant, talking to the Lord.

Sometimes, I felt like a new man. But I wasn't. I was still smoking crack. I wasn't stealing as much, but honestly, that didn't have much to do with God. We were in a long-term lay-up, and that's not conducive to petty theft, because you have to steal, steal, steal to survive on shoplifting, and the stores get to know you pretty quick. I wasn't earning my keep, in other words, and when you're a crackhead couple with a long-term understanding, one partner not earning his keep won't sit well with the other.

Kathy tolerated it for a while. She even took to praying because it was an activity we could do together. But eventually she tired of my lounging, because it meant she had to work harder, and she took out her frustration on my spirituality. "You pray over your food, but smoke crack," she said with disgust. "You think that's gonna get you off the street?"

Give up crack if you're so serious about your religion, that was the implication. But give up praying, that was the real meaning. Give up the prayers, Kathy was saying, because I know you're not giving up your addiction.

It made me angry, her lack of faith. But my choices made me even angrier. I was doing wrong. I was failing twenty, thirty times a day, and I knew it. It was on me—all on me. But I blamed Kathy, because that was the easy thing to do. I said her lifestyle was bringing me down, even though it was supporting my habit, and I started to berate her for the choices she made.

"Oh, you don't like prostitution," she said. "That's funny, because you still like crack."

"Oh, you don't like stealing. Well, how about getting a job instead?"

She had followed my lead for a while. She had tried to walk in the ways of God. We'd even talked about rehab, although neither of us was ready. But when I started blaming her, being holier-than-thou, the relationship fell apart. She talked back, I got angry, and we fought. I think she wanted to break me, wanted to send me back to the sorry place I'd been for so many years, because she was trying so hard, she was hustling all day, every day, and it wasn't enough. Not for the both of us.

Then she stumbled on a scam. There was a night clerk at one of the motels, a socially awkward guy. She had strung him along for months, made him fantasize about her, showed him just enough to whet his appetite. I mean, he was making maybe thirty thousand a year, tops, and she took him for a few hundred dollars before finally, one day, taking him into the office behind the front desk counter.

It was over in two seconds, but she had him then. Now it wasn't the promise of sex, it was the threat of exposure. "Give me everything in your wallet, or I'll tell your boss what happened."

When he stopped bringing money to work, it was, "Two hundred dollars tomorrow or I'm telling everything. *Everything.*"

The guy shook like a leaf when he saw her coming. He sweated through his shirt. I saw him break down in tears on several occasions. "Please. Please leave me alone. I don't have anything else."

In our old life, it would have been just another way to get through the day. But this time, it felt bad. Real bad. The poor guy was weak, and Kathy took advantage. She got him in her grip, and she squeezed. He gave us money. He gave us free rooms. He let Kathy into the employee lounge, where she even stole the loose change left in a wicker basket for sodas and chips.

I said, "Maybe we should let him go."

"Hell, no."

I didn't argue. I felt guilty, I was torn up inside, but I didn't stop. Many times, I smoked that young man's money. Many times, I sat in his free motel room, blasting rocks. Kathy's going to read this and say, "You're making me look heartless, Ted. I feel bad about that, too." And she does. Now. She's taken off her armor, and she feels terribly guilty now. But at the time, she wasn't guilty. She was gleeful, not about the poor sucker—I think she probably felt bad about him even then—but about my hypocrisy. She had been *afraid* of what I was capable of, but she wasn't worried now. I'd suggest rehab, and instead of arguing, she'd laugh. "You're never going away," she said. "Don't even pretend you are."

At the beginning of our relationship, I was the hard one, although my protective skin was made out of humor and hugs. But somewhere on our journey, we'd crossed each other. Somewhere along the line, Kathy became the hard one, and the more I tried to walk in the ways of God, even though I was failing miserably, the more apparent that became.

Eventually, the scam ended. She let the motel clerk go. We went back to our Mexican restaurant squat. By the time the police finally came to roust us, I had made a decision. I knew we were going back to our old life—burning out whole blocks by stealing six or seven times a day, crashing in alleys and crack houses, robbing johns in motel rooms—and I didn't want to do it anymore. But Kathy was locked in. She was hopeless, and therefore she was a lifer. So there was only one thing to do.

I decided to quit Kathy for good.

Kathy

Ted kept talking about rehab. He wanted me to go to Marysville, the state-run treatment center. I wouldn't do it. I didn't want to stop smoking, that's true. But more importantly, I didn't want to leave Ted. Marysville was women only, so I would have to go alone. And Ted would leave me. That's what I believed, and I was more addicted to him than the crack.

So, no, I didn't hate his spirituality. I didn't hate his desire to get clean. I wanted that, too. But to me, at that time, it was the hammer Ted was using to break us. After I cleaned up, I thought that was crack sickness. I thought it was paranoia. But reading this book, I see it was true. And I don't know . . . that late in our relationship, it sort of breaks my heart.

But we couldn't go on, not like before. We were fighting. We were hateful. We were tired in body and soul. My bones were nothing but toothpicks. They were so fragile, I couldn't run. I know Ted took a fall for me. During one heist, he turned back and confronted a clerk so I could get away. They caught him and sent him up for a few weeks, his last arrest. I was broken by that. I was tough on the outside, because I had to be, but I was broken inside.

I needed Ted. I had to hold on to him, and I knew that kind of weakness would drive him away.

I was thinking along those lines, desperate lines, when I noticed a middle-aged man standing out by some gas pumps. He was a good-looking guy, wearing cutoff jeans and flip-flops. He looked like a dad. But he was talking to every person at the pumps, and some of them were taking him to an ATM next door, and some of them were giving him money out of their wallets.

So I introduced myself. He told me his car had broken down, and he was trying to get money to fix it. I knew that wasn't true, so I watched him. Sure enough, he was back the next day. Eventually, he told me the truth. He was a crack addict. He lived in a flop a few blocks away. He had a crack-addict girlfriend, too. They were nice people. Ted and I ended up staying with them for about a month.

When we moved on to another part of town, I stole his hustle. It took me a while to perfect it, but after a few weeks I developed a pitch. I walked up to someone at the gas pump, or caught them coming out of the gas station store, and said:

> Pardon me. How are you? Is there any way you can help me and my dad and daughter and son? We are so stranded. We are on our way to Akron and my credit card is not working. We have no cash, we have been stranded for about eight hours on the freeway, and we have called the police and the only thing they can do is call a tow truck, which will cost us hundreds and hundreds of dollars. I am a Christian. Is there any possible way you can help us with anything at all, and I would gladly send it back to you?

I could con ten to twenty dollars pretty easily. Occasionally, I'd get a hundred. If they offered me a ride, I'd call Ted, who was always nearby. They didn't like seeing a man—it raised the danger factor—but he was such a gentleman, he disarmed them pretty quick.

"I'm going to Akron to apply for a radio job," Ted told them. That was his line. "Do you think I have what it takes?"

Oh, they loved him. I mean, that voice, what's not to love? They'd chat away, encouraging him and his radio career, telling him he was a special talent, and more often than not I'd steal a few extra dollars from their wallet. Sometimes, we'd convince them to drive us across town and drop us off at a convenient spot.

"Our car's around the corner," Ted would tell them, "but it's not a nice area. Why don't you just drop us off here?"

They were more than happy not to drive two strangers into a bad neighborhood. We were more than happy to thank them, take their address, promise to pray for them and let them know if Ted got that radio job in Akron. I think most of those people, to this day, think they offered Christian charity to good, hardworking people in need. But of course it wasn't our car around the corner. It was a crack house; and their money was gone before they left town.

It was a miracle, really. The con was so easy. And safe. So safe. These were ordinary people. They weren't going to pull a gun. They weren't going to beat or rape me. They weren't going to turn us in to the cops. It was perfect, really: the right scam at the right time. For a while, I thought it would save us. I thought conning people at gas stations was the answer to my prayers.

CHAPTER 22

was boxed in. I know that sounds strange for a guy whose world was so small, but I didn't know where to turn. Kathy's new con, in a way, was an ideal solution. We were suffering, and we needed something low-stress to carry us into the next phase of our addiction. The old Ted Williams would have jumped at the opportunities.

But the new Ted Williams? That wasn't the way I wanted to go. When Kathy said "I'm a Christian," it turned my stomach upside down. It felt worse, even though it wasn't, than the motel clerk. It's one thing to con men who hire prostitutes; I justified that for years. I justified stealing from stores by telling myself it didn't hurt nobody, although Kathy's sister Colleen, who owned a famous local store called Colleen's Collectibles (where I shoplifted several times), disagreed. She always told me, "It's people like you who drive up my taxes. It's people like you who drive up my insurance." Colleen was not a big Ted Williams fan.

But conning good, hardworking Christians? Preying on average citizens? And lying about God to do it? That was something else entirely.

Acknowledge Him.

I talked with God all the time. I acknowledged Him. I promised Him I'd improve my behavior. I promised to attend church once a week, and I was working up the courage to try. So when Kathy said "I'm a Christian," that was technically true. We believed in Jesus. We both prayed to Him. But the reason she mentioned it . . . the way she said it to achieve something in return . . . that turned the truth into a lie.

"Well, what do you want to do, Ted?"

Acknowledge Him. "I don't know."

"You think stealing is better?"

In all your ways. "I don't know."

"You think hooking is better?"

Acknowledge Him. "I don't know."

"Do you want to quit smoking? Are you really ready for rehab?"

I was quiet on that one. "No."

Sobriety was the way out of my relationship with Kathy. It was the way off the street. I knew that, I prayed for that strength, but I couldn't commit. I couldn't leave the life. And I couldn't get Kathy to commit either, which in my twisted mind would have been just as good, because she'd have been gone.

But I don't think, in my heart, I wanted Kathy to leave. If I had, I wouldn't have fought with her. I wouldn't have tried so hard to change her. I would have walked away, because walking away was easy. I'd been walked away from all my life.

Acknowledge Him.

So no rehab, but less sin. That left one other option. One other idea swirling around my crack-addled brain. But even as I pondered my future, even as I prayed about it, I refused to hear the voice. It was a murmur, I told myself, so I couldn't understand it. I'd talk to

God, and my thoughts would touch on the idea, and I'd tell myself, *Keep it together, Ted, don't go crazy now. Don't do something stupid.* I heard the suggestion, but I didn't know if it was God or the devil or crack residue in my brain. I didn't know if this idea was the end or the beginning, the last chance or the last step down to the bottom of the hole.

"One hour," the voice said.

But I shook my head no. I couldn't go that low. Even when pushed, I couldn't take that step. I could offer lip service, that's all. Lip service had been the subject of my Jehovah's Witness testimony on the day I was caught smoking. "In the words of the Lord," my talk would have concluded, "people honor me with their lips, but their hearts are far removed." Thirty years later, that's what I was doing. I was saying the right words, but my heart was afraid.

Acknowledge Him, Ted.

And then, one day, I remembered the last part of my Bible verse. It wasn't "all your ways." There was more. The Bible said, Acknowledge Him in all your ways, *and He shall direct your path.*

CHAPTER 23

Kathy wasn't happy. "God is telling you to beg on the street corner?"

She didn't believe me, and she didn't understand. Why, she asked, why would I take myself out of the game, willingly, and in the worst possible way? Why, after fifteen years of partnership, would I choose to embarrass her? Everyone knew Ted Williams was Kathy's man, nobody even knew us apart anymore, and she didn't want her man standing on the corner . . . begging. Of all things—begging! Like a d*mn homeless man.

I wasn't too happy either. In fact, I hated the idea. It was humiliating. Homeless people who stood on the side of the road and asked for money were bums, the lowest form of humanity. Everybody knew that. Even crackheads looked down on them, because they had no pride. They weren't asking for sympathy or human decency, they were asking for pity, pure and simple.

You're not Radio, a voice inside me said. *You're Ted Williams, the Golden Voice. You used to be somebody. Ted Williams don't beg.*

I said, "No, Lord, not that. Anything but that."

His golden voice replied, "You offered a day. I'm asking for an hour."

I heard that truth. For months, I had promised God I would take Sundays off, observe a day of cleanliness and gratitude, in a church if I could, but at the very least without crack. But for months, I had failed. Now the voice was relieving me of that promise, and asking for only one clean hour in return.

Acknowledge Him.

"I have to do it, Kathy."

He will direct your path.

I chose the exit at Hudson Street and I-71, a few miles north of downtown Columbus. Nothing moral or God-directed about that decision. We were laying up with a low-level drug dealer named Mark at the time, and that intersection was only a short walk away.

So that was two big decisions made. First, to do it. Second, to do it there. My next task was making a sign. I didn't want to just ask for money, or write the same thing as everyone else. *Homeless vet. Hungry. Need work.* Those things were true, but they weren't the truth. I was a homeless vet, but my army service didn't put me on the street. I needed work, but honestly, I didn't want a job. Standing on the corner was my work, and maybe you can't understand that, but I can assure you of this: It was all the work I could handle at that time.

I didn't want anonymity, a sentence to hide behind. Once I accepted the idea of going public, I wanted to go all the way. I wanted drivers to see me, to know me, so they'd understand they were giving to a real human being, someone with his own past, dreams, and, obviously, failures. I needed people to know I had a gift, a true honest gift that made me worthwhile: my voice.

So I described myself from the heart.

I HAVE A GOD-GIVEN GIFT OF VOICE. I AM AN
EX-RADIO ANNOUNCER WHO HAS FALLEN

ON HARD TIMES. PLEASE. ANY HELP WILL BE
GREATLY APPRECIATED. GOD BLESS.

I took my sign to the corner. It wasn't that day. It wasn't the next day. I think it took maybe a week before I summoned the courage to walk all the way to the highway. There was a Wendy's on the east side of the exit, and an abandoned BP gas station with a nice shaded place to sit, so it was a good spot. But there were two or three homeless people already there. That was their corner, clearly, because they beat me to it, and on the street, finders-keepers was the primary rule.

I gave them a smile when I finally walked past. "How you doing?" I said, waving. They watched me without a word. They were fifty feet or so off the road, on the shady curb in front of the former convenience store, so I couldn't see the expression on their faces, but I knew they weren't happy. Nobody's happy to see a new salesman in the territory.

I walked across the highway overpass to the west-side median, on the southbound exit ramp. I took a deep breath. The light turned red. *Acknowledge Him.*

"This is it, Lord," I said, looking to the sky.

I held up my sign and looked at the ground. Then I looked in the window of the car stopped right in front of me at the light. The woman wasn't looking at me. Nobody in the line of cars was looking at me. They were aware of me, I could tell, but they were looking the other way, or fiddling with the radio, pretending I wasn't there.

After an hour, I'd only made a dollar, which was terrible, *terrible*, except it wasn't an hour, it was about seven minutes. But it felt like seven days. I said, "God, I don't want to do this."

He didn't say anything. I started to feel joy in my heart, like He was letting me go, and then . . .

I thought of my momma. I thought of her words: "Don't come home, son. It's not going to work. Don't come home." I thought of the promise I'd made to God, to get off the street before she died. To make her proud one time.

She'd hate me for standing here begging. I knew that. Momma would hate me for embarrassing her. I mean, I hate myself for it. But it was the only way.

I turned back to the cars. I tried not to think about it, but I could see the way some people looked at me, like I was garbage, like I polluted their view. Their looks brought back Momma's words, after I missed my father's funeral: *How dare you.*

After an hour, I trudged back toward Mark's house. There was an old white man out on the east corner with a sign, a beat-to-hell nose, and a faded blue tattoo of a marijuana leaf on his chest. I knew he was one of the homeless men, out now to catch the afternoon rush.

"I got three dollars."

He looked at me and snuffled. "Your sign's too long," he said.

He was right. I saw drivers trying to read it, then speeding off because the light changed before they were through. I remember a black dude walking down the median toward me, which was un- usual, because the median was a strip of grass on the highway side of the exit, and nobody ever walked there. He came right up to me, read my sign, and said, "Golden voice, huh? Let me hear you sing."

"No, I'm an ex-radio announcer."

He read the sign again. "Oh. Well, say something, then."

"When you're listening to nothing but the best of oldies, you're listen- ing to Magic 98.9."

"Dang, man," he said, stepping back to eye my ratty hair and brown teeth. "You're good. What you doing out here on the street? You should be working in radio."

Then he stuck his hands in his pockets and shuffled on, leaving me with the truth of those words.

Even the cop agreed my sign was a disgrace. "You need a shorter message, buddy. Nobody's going to read your life story." He told me this on the third or fourth day, while he was tearing up my sign. He handed it back to me, along with a ticket. "Have a nice day," he said.

I went to court. The fine was sixty-five dollars for panhandling.

I told the judge, "Where am I going to get sixty-five dollars? I'll have to panhandle for it."

She was a sour judge. She wasn't amused.

I trudged back home, feeling lower than before. *Why, God?* I wondered. *Why?*

I stole the money for the fine, of course. Kathy and I were still stealing, because, well, I was clean for an hour on the corner, but the rest of the day I was still on crack. There was a tug-of-war, not only between my heart and my addiction but between Kathy and me over the direction of our partnership. She wanted to keep going, even though we were doomed. I wanted out.

I knew there was good in her, because I'd been there myself, in a stuck position, only a few months before. She worked the area around Hudson Street and I-71, whoring and using her broken-down-car scam, and I knew that scam ate her up inside—I knew it—but she couldn't change. There was a Speedway gas station half a block from my corner, and I watched her one afternoon working the con on an older woman. The lady handed her some money, then turned away, and in a split second Kathy reached into her purse and grabbed more money. I saw her stuff it into her bra, but I wasn't the only one. Someone else saw her, too, and she was detained after a brief scuffle. The cops frisked her, roughly as usual, stuck their hands down in her bra and practically ripped it off, treated her like garbage, but they couldn't find the money, so they reluctantly let her go.

She sauntered up to me, smiling, knowing I'd watched the whole thing. She sat down, took off her sock, and showed me two hundred dollars. She was a master. That was a slick trick in a sticky situation, especially with her long criminal record. But instead of congratulating her, I just shook my head.

I saw the look in her eyes. She knew it was wrong. That's what kept me with her, I think. She wanted to go straight, she wanted to follow in the ways of the Lord, but she was in so deep. She needed me to take her hand and lead.

So I looked her right in the eye, and I said, "Let's go."

I led her straight to Mark's house, and we bought two hundred dollars' worth of crack. I should have told her to give back the money. The old woman was gone, but she could have turned it over to the police, or maybe a charity. At the very least, I should have kept my hands off. But I didn't. Instead, I spent another long afternoon and evening blasting off to the clouds.

Kathy loved that. She would have loved for me to set a good example even more, but this was the next best thing: self-righteous Teddy, *her same old Teddy*, wallowing in his greed. I was a hypocrite, that's what Kathy always thought. That's why it took so long for her to believe in me. And in a way, she was right. Here I was, a crack-head, smoking every day, stealing, blasting off with money my girl-friend made from robbing old ladies, and I was proud because I no longer said g*dd*mn? Because I spent one measly hour a day clean, begging for the Lord?

But that one hour was so hard. It almost killed me, day after day, to see those people drive by with hate, or disgust, or pity in their eyes. It was hard to watch my own children (one of whom lived nearby) drive by and turn away, so they didn't have to acknowledge me.

It was hard to see Kathy's sister drive by every few days and stare at me, with her window closed, and not say a word. It was hard to know that she didn't even need to come by that intersection; it wasn't near her house or her store. It was as if she came by anyway just to rub it in.

So we fought. Kathy and I—we fought like dogs that summer of 2010 and into the fall. Don't get me wrong, we'd fought a lot over the years. When you're in a relationship with someone for fourteen years, you're going to fight, especially if you've got crack between you, and you're living a life of crime on the streets. House repairs? Life fulfillment? Where to send the kids to kindergarten? We didn't have those arguments, but we fought about money, about who smoked what, about who was forced to commit the crimes.

But these fights were different. I was desperate to get away, not just from Kathy but from my life, and she was even more desperate to keep me. She was tenacious, always had been, especially when she knew what she wanted. She didn't show me any more affection, but she fought like hell to keep me in the only way she knew how, by holding her ground, by making me hate her, because when you hate, at least, you're showing you care.

Then it happened. An argument escalated, I don't even remember what it was about, but it was no doubt the same argument we'd been having for months. Like always, the words became harsher and harsher, round after round, until finally Kathy found the right words to hurt me—"You black gay n*gger"—and in an instant, without a thought, I slapped her to the ground.

She fell to her knees. Kathy was a ferocious woman. She was as hard as stone. But she was so weak, less than ninety pounds with bones like toothpicks, and it wasn't hard to knock her down. When I hit her, she crumpled. She lay in a heap, quiet, with her head down.

Then she looked at me, and I saw vulnerability in her eyes. I saw that little girl she'd once been, maybe, a long time ago. She said, "How can you call yourself a Christian? How can you call yourself a Christian when you beat me to the ground?"

Kathy

I don't know why I said it. I don't know why I broke down. I was trying so hard. I was working so hard to keep us together. But I was tired. I was sick. I was lonely and scared. Scared I was going to lose him. Scared I was going to die alone in my addiction.

It wasn't planned. I wasn't crying for my mother or my brother, or my lost life, or even the pain. I was crying for Ted, because I thought it was over for sure.

Then I looked up, and I saw him looking down at me, and I knew something was different. He didn't look angry. He didn't look self-righteous. He looked . . . hurt. By what he'd done. He turned away. He didn't say another word. But I knew. He hated his actions like he'd never hated them before.

All I'd ever wanted was for Ted to love me. All I'd ever wanted was his loyalty and respect. All I'd ever wanted, really, was to be treated kind.

Yes, I hated Ted's Christianity. I fought with him over it, because I thought it was a con. But that slap. That look. It took away my anger. It took away my fear. It opened my heart. Just a little bit at first. Just a crack. Because I realized, after fourteen years with Ted, after forty-nine years on earth . . . I'd found what I was searching for.

CHAPTER 24

L ife got a little easier after the fight with Kathy because I took responsibility, I stopped blaming my girlfriend for my sins. My heart felt lighter, and I felt like I was more in control.

But that didn't make the corner any easier, and there were bad days that autumn, many hard days. There were days when it rained. Days when rednecks threw half-full cans of Coke at me or a black man flipped a cigarette butt at my head. There were days when young men signaled me over to their window and said, "Get a job, n*gger," then laughed as they drove away. (There were Ohio State football game days, too—the best days of all.) There were days when I prayed, "Lord, take me away from here. Just take me away." I didn't mean to a better place, I meant the crack house.

If I worked fifteen minutes and didn't receive a dime, I said, "Lord, this ain't my day. Let me go, and I promise you, I'll be back tomorrow."

Sometimes, a voice replied, *All right, Ted, put down that sign, have a hit, you've done enough today.*

I'd turn around, happiness in my heart. Then I'd think of my momma and all her pain over the years. I'd think of Kathy, and how

I'd taken her for granted, and how much I owed her—I almost said loved, but I think *owed* is better. I'd think about how far I'd come, about all the corners I'd turned, and I'd think, *Wait a second, Ted, that wasn't the Lord, that was the devil. That was selfishness leading you astray.*

I'd turn back around, hold up my sign, and think, *Acknowledge Him, Ted. Acknowledge Him in all your WAYS.* That's what the verse said, and the last word was important. Ways meant actions. It wasn't my prayer that acknowledged God, it was being on that corner. For that one hour every day, I was acknowledging Him.

I can't say that for the other twenty-three hours I was a moral person. I still smoked crack every day. But I was using less, and that's the truth. By October, I was smoking maybe fifty dollars a day in dope, instead of a hundred, and I'd like to lay that on God, but it was primarily because I didn't have the money for more. It turns out poverty was the best way short of rehab to curb my twenty-year addiction.

Life wasn't a scramble either, like it had been before. Most days, Kathy and I laid up with our drug dealer Mark. This wasn't a crack house situation; Mark was strictly small-time. He was on disability, but that only covered his rent, so he dealt to a few customers to make ends meet. He didn't have the best dope, but he was a notorious Captain Save-a-Ho, as we called them on the street. He liked helping dopeheads. A former prostitute had been living with him for years. No sex, nothing like that. Mark was overweight and diabetic, and he rarely left his house. She was his personal nurse, running his errands and taking care of his medical needs, which kept her off the street. That may not sound like a charitable service, a free maid in exchange for drugs, but her life was better with Mark, and ours was, too.

Twenty dollars a night pay-to-lay, that was the arrangement for a bed in the basement; and Mark was easy with credit so my panhandling usually paid the "rent." Kathy turned tricks for a few bucks more. The rest we made off stealing. We stole a DVD player one day from a store I could see from my panhandling corner (that was my life, the good and the bad, within a few hundred feet of each other), and we were out on Hudson a few hours later trying to sell it. A man drove up and said, "Let me see that."

Kathy handed the DVD player to the man, he looked it over . . . and sped away. Kathy was livid. She chased him down the street, and of course that didn't work, so she came back huffing. "I can't believe that bastard stole from us," she said with that hard look, the one that made me feel she was capable of anything.

In the past, I'd have been livid, too, because that DVD player meant crack. But that time, I don't know, the theft felt right. "Well, we stole it first," I said. "Who are we to complain?"

That was my new understanding of the world, that everything was a balance. My daily sins would be punished, but my good deeds would be rewarded, too. It was progress, not perfection. It was a matter of tipping the scale, of doing more good in the world than bad.

For the first time in years, I started eating. At first, I had hated when drivers gave me food, because what was I going to do with a half-eaten bag of potato chips or the apple those skinny bagel-eating college girls always handed me, saying, "I've eaten enough. I don't need more." I was so paranoid, I thought a homeless-hater might try to poison me. But it wasn't long before I ate the handouts. The less I smoked, the hungrier I became, until I looked forward to those skinny sorority girls in their peppy cars. I even bought food and cooked for Kathy from time to time, sharing the meal with Mark as well, in exchange for using his kitchen.

When tempers flared, either with Mark or Kathy, I spent time on the corner. I hadn't been welcomed at first, and it wasn't just wariness of the new guy. The regulars on Hudson and I-71 were mostly alcoholics, not crackheads, and they had the classic look of the homeless: red watery eyes, bulbous noses, tattered clothes, and pockmarked skin. Three or four of them, depending on the day, lived in two tents in the ten-foot-wide weedy bushes along the highway median. The back tent was a traditional camp. The front one, about six paces back from the Dumpster area of the abandoned gas station, was a blue tarp with a trampled space in front and garbage strewn in the bushes. That's what I showed the television cameras, after I became the most famous homeless man in America and the whole country wanted to see "my corner." But that wasn't my tent, it was only a place I slept when Mark kicked me out for the night. It was Vic's tent, and it took me weeks to gain access. Like the other homeless on the corner, Vic resented the fact that I disappeared every night and came back clean. Clean was a relative term, of course, but they thought I was a fake. In other words: I wasn't successful enough for the real world, but I wasn't homeless enough for theirs.

Over time, though, I became a member of the group. I brought them things every now and then, a cigarette or some chili from the Wendy's next door, which we all loved. *Wendy's cheesy chili, the choice of the homeless man*, can't you just hear the Golden Voice saying that in a commercial right now? We ate it almost every day, sitting in front of the boarded-up gas station, and over time Vic and I became friends.

We kept an eye on each other when we were working our corners, because there's always a threat of violence. I was walking down Hudson one day and a man jumped out of a car and punched me in the face, knocking me down. Then he kicked me twice, jumped back in his car, and sped away. Vic and I tried to warn each other about those kinds of people: the angry ones, the ones looking for trouble. We even worked out a system for the cops. We'd signal whenever we saw a police car approaching, then we'd run into the bushes on opposite sides of the road.

One day, a driver rolled down her window and handed me paper money, the best feeling in the world. I thanked her sincerely, said, "God bless you, ma'am, God bless you," and smiled as she drove away.

Two dollars! *Thank you, Jesus*, I acknowledged.

Then I looked down in my hand. It wasn't two dollars; it was two twenty-dollar bills. Oh, my heart leapt. I yelled, "Thank you, Jesus!" right out loud. It was all I could do to stand on the corner the rest of my hour, because the thought of crack was circling my mind. *Forty dollars. Two rocks. Two rocks!* With my new diminished habit, it was enough to last the rest of the day.

When the hour rolled around, I jumped off that corner. I was walking on air as I headed over the bridge. About halfway across I spotted Vic on his corner. He was standing with his sign, and I could tell by the way his shoulders slouched he was having a hard day. I was in such a good mood, so jazzed by that woman's generosity, that I went up to Vic and handed him one of the twenties. "For you, brother," I said.

Oh, man. I felt good then. I thought, *Ted Williams. Now that's the real Ted Williams right there.*

Of course, that night, high on crack, I started mourning that twenty dollars. I wanted it back for crack . . . and I'm sorry, God, but that was Ted Williams right there, too.

CHAPTER 25

I was part of a community on the corner, the first I'd been a part of in years. It went beyond Kathy, and beyond even the homeless men and women at the abandoned BP. It extended to the owner of Wasserstein Kitchen Appliances, who invited me to eat his promotional popcorn when I was hungry. It included the employees from Continental Office Environments, who, after watching me poke around their outdoor ashtray for good cigarette butts for a few weeks, started giving me spare change and dollar bills. The employees at Speedway took Kathy in. She had gone mostly straight, begging from people at the pumps, but telling them honestly that she was a longtime drug addict and prostitute trying to go clean. The employees, instead of kicking her off the property, started giving her the old pizza from the warmer and other foods they were otherwise going to throw away.

And then there were my regulars. Many of the people who drove by my corner became a part of my life, because I saw them every day. More than once, someone rolled down the window and said, "Remember me?"

"Yes, ma'am," I said, because I always remembered faces. "You gave me a dollar yesterday, and I appreciate it."

Sometimes they slowed down, even if the light wasn't red, and yelled, "I'm getting paid tomorrow. I'll have a little something for you then."

"God bless you," I yelled back, because I knew they were telling the truth. The people in the Mercedes, they weren't giving. If I saw a nice car, I just smiled, because that was a waste of time. In my experience, no rich person ever gave to a homeless man. But the working-class people . . . so many working-class people gave, even though they didn't have much.

Then there were the Christian ladies, the ones who rolled down their windows and said, "God loves you, son. God loves you." Some didn't give me anything, and I thought, *Is that His love?*

Some said, "I'm praying for you," then rolled up their windows, and I thought, *Well, don't, because you won't even touch my hand.*

Others gave me the change out of their purses, and God help me, I smiled and chatted with them, but I looked at their cars disappearing through the intersection and thought, *Is that all?*

One woman came by every few days, and always looked me in the eye like a fellow human being, and always said the same thing. "I'm going to give you this five-dollar bill, and I'm not going to tell you what to do with it, but I hope you spend it right, because God loves you."

I spent most of that money on crack, of course, and I know that wonderful woman will be disappointed if she reads this. But what she said, even more than the money, made a difference to me. She wasn't judging me, and she wasn't telling me what to do. I think about her words all the time, even now, because they came from such an open heart. She wasn't giving with demands. She wasn't expecting anything in return.

Acknowledge Him.

A man once gave my buddy Vic a five-dollar bill. Vic took the money to Rodney's for malt liquor, because Vic was an alcoholic, and when he came out the door, the man was standing in the parking lot. "I knew it," the man said, pointing a finger in his face. "I knew it. You said you were hungry, but you're using my money on booze. I knew you were no good."

Well, I say if you have hate like that in your heart, don't give. If strings are attached, don't give, because I can't tell you what I'm spending your money on, because I don't know.

Acknowledge Him.

I was a better person by October 2010, but that was hard for the world to see. Drivers still passed me with a sneer. Some managers of nearby businesses still cursed me and drove me off their property. My kids didn't want me in their homes, and when I did manage to wangle a visit, I still always managed to somehow let them down. Kathy's sister Colleen still drove by every few days and gave me the eye without rolling down her window or saying a word.

I called my momma. I said, "Momma, do you still make those beans with potatoes?"

"Yes, I do."

"Momma, I've been missing those beans and potatoes."

"Don't come home, Ted. It's not going to work."

But that woman in the car—she saw me. She accepted me. She accepted that I might do wrong, but she never stopped reaching out. And what she really gave me, her faith and hope, affected my life. *Acknowledge.* It made me want to be a better person. *Acknowledge.* It showed me the kindness and mercy that existed in the world.

And even though I took her money to Mark, her faith sustained me. It made me proud that I was smoking less. That I was fighting with Kathy less. That I was stealing less and working off a lot of my debts by running errands for Mark or by keeping him company while he waited in line to pay his electric bill.

Of course, there was some stealing, too. Mark would say, "That new Jay-Z album coming out. You think you can get me a copy?"

Or, "It's getting cold, Ted. I could use a jacket. I got my eye on one like this."

Mark was a well-read man. He'd been a reader all his life, but he learned about black empowerment during a ten-year prison stint, and after that he read every black author from W. E. B. DuBois to Terry McMillan. He wasn't into sports, although we did talk LeBron, because LeBron was about to screw Ohio big-time, and that's what everybody talked about. But more often, we talked about Richard Wright and Ralph Ellison's *Invisible Man* and *Waiting to Exhale*. I didn't read those books, mind you, I stole them, because Mark loved books about the black man and woman.

He talked to me about them, too. He talked to me about Malcolm and Martin and Precious, the fat black girl from the ghetto created by a black girl from the suburbs—and after a while I started feeling better about myself. I started to see success, started to realize my brothers and sisters made a difference in the world. I guess I finally realized the black race didn't have to be low, as my father always said.

Of course, a black man had been elected president of the United States, so any fool should have been able to see that, but I didn't have a connection to the culture, didn't watch TV, never touched a computer, or heard the latest music. Mark gave me a little space, though, where I didn't have to hustle, and that helped a little cultural light shine in.

Mark was also a recovering addict, having gotten clean in prison, so he knew my struggles. Whether we were talking Sapphire or the price of dope, he always shook his head when I bent over the pipe and said, "You got to pray, Radio. You got to go down on your knees. It's the only way."

"I know, Mark. I know. I'm praying my ass off. I'm sorry, Lord, I mean I'm praying my . . . I'm praying hard every night."

That's the contradiction: a drug dealer helping me get clean but also pushing me to steal for his crack. A safe space to stop hustling, but it's the same space where I smoked. Finding self-worth through service to God on a street corner, but that service making me look more worthless than ever.

That's the street, really, that give-and-take. Morality might seem nice and tidy from a comfortable living room, with a paycheck and health insurance and . . . a toilet, but when you're trying to make do, trying to break the habits of a lifetime, things aren't so neat. Beg so as not to steal, steal so as not to hunger, con a little so you don't lie a lot. Go straight with the help of a criminal, understand the absurdity of the situation but do it anyway, take the chance, because it's your last best shot.

I couldn't have made it if I'd taken Al Battle's offer of free rent. Every time I backslid—and, brother, I backslid a lot over those months—I'd have been tormented. I remember stealing a bottle of alcohol during a recording session at a studio that autumn, then slipping out onto the fire escape to drink it. When I walked back in, Al and the producer were staring at me. "You don't have to do that, Ted," Al said. "If you ask, you can have what you need."

He was right, I didn't *have* to do that. But I did. Over and over again, I shamed myself, and I let myself down. If I'd have done it too much with Al Battle, I'd have lost his friendship, and then I'd have lost my last link to radio.

With Mark, though, there was no pressure, because Mark really wasn't my friend. He used me for my habit, charging me for everything from the bed to the crack to the water, which was why I rarely showered. Kathy showered almost every day, she was scrupulous about her appearance, but I couldn't stomach the thought of paying for water, so I avoided them, let myself get dirty and my Afro stand on end.

I was happy, in my way. I was making it work. But I wasn't quite believing. I guess that's the best way of putting it: I wasn't sure this path was going to lead me out. I had so many issues to deal with, so many flaws. I was angry. I was entitled. I was impatient, especially on those hard days when it was raining and nobody was stopping—and the hunger for crack was on me like an extra skin. By late October, after three months on the corner, I needed something good to happen. I'd worked three months on faith, and my strength was low. I needed a sign of progress to help me go on.

That something turned out to be a phone call. And it wasn't even a phone call for me. It was for Kathy, and it came from her sister Colleen.

What did Colleen say?

She invited Kathy shopping.

The next day, they went to the grocery store. In the past, Kathy would have bought as much as she could, then sold it for drugs, but we had changed our ways. Kathy was eating, she was keeping her blood sugar more normal, so we treated the food in the usual way: we ate it.

But it wasn't the food that mattered. It was Colleen's trust. After ten years of a broken relationship, Kathy's older sister was reaching out. There were a few bumps—on their second trip together, to a gas station to buy cigarettes, the clerk kicked Kathy out because he recognized her as a thief—but the relationship kept building. This was the first gesture her family had made in years, and believe me, I'm not blaming them—we burned their trust to the ground, we robbed Colleen's store, we lied and stole, we made it impossible for them to love us or even have us around.

But Colleen loved us anyway.

When she invited us to her house for dinner, that was . . . I get teary-eyed thinking about it, because to be accepted back into Colleen's home . . . to be trusted . . . that meant the world to Kathy. That was the moment, I think, that opened her heart and changed her life.

It meant the world to me, too, because I knew why Colleen had invited us. I knew, finally, why she had been driving by my corner for so many months. She had been watching, and for the first time in a long time, she had seen some good in me.

CHAPTER 26

There were still a lot of issues to work through. Anger. Impatience. And most of all, entitlement, a problem all my life. I expected the army to put me in communications, even though I didn't qualify. I expected radio stations to coddle me, even though I abused their trust. I expected Patty to give me the freedom I wanted, even when I ran from responsibility. I expected my father to love me for who I was, even when I defied his rules.

And I wanted the world to open up to me on that corner . . . right now. I even complained about it to God. I said, *This should get easier, Lord. The more I stand here, the more money I should get. The more I tip the balance toward the good, the more rewards, isn't that our deal?*

The longer I stood on the corner, the more I started to feel drivers owed me, like it was their obligation to give me spare change just because I was coming faithfully every day. I started to feel like those Christian women who said "God loves you" were sinning, somehow, because they owed me more. What was fifty cents to them? What was a dollar? It was nothing. But it was everything to me, because it wasn't just my livelihood, it was validation of my new life.

That sense of entitlement made me frustrated, so frustrated, especially on bad days when I stayed three hours for a few bucks, and especially as winter began to set in. I came off the corner one cold day after a bad hour, maybe a quarter in my pocket, and I saw a woman handing Vic a twenty-dollar bill.

So I walked over to him. "Hey, Vic, remember when I shared that forty dollars with you a few weeks back?"

He looked away. "Nah, Ted."

"I gave you twenty, man. I'm just asking for ten."

He looked further away. "No," he mumbled. "I don't think so."

Brothers and sisters, I was angry, because that wasn't fair, that wasn't right, where was my reward for doing good, Lord? Where was my return?

I was halfway down the block before I realized how wrong I was. *Ted,* I said to myself, *you didn't give from the heart.* When I shared that money with Vic, I didn't expect anything back, because I was in a good mood that day, I was rolling high. But now that I was down, I wanted it back, and that, I realized, undid all the good. That wasn't nothing but selfishness in another form.

Acknowledge.

Lord, help me be a better person, I prayed.

I knew what I needed to do. I knew the person I needed to be. But there were days, brothers and sisters, there were days. After months of smoking less, I was starting to crave, and there were days I felt like peeling off my skin. There were days I didn't want to look at myself, because I still didn't like what I saw, and because I couldn't avoid the indictment in drivers' eyes: loser, taker, bum.

As the cold wind of November pushed me into Thanksgiving and into memories of my family—my children, Patty, Momma, even my father—I grew resentful, not just in my mind but in my heart. I watched cars drive by and wondered, *Why won't those people help me?*

Why can't they see how hard it is to stand before them? This was my service to the Lord, my path to salvation. A dollar was nothing to them, but a dollar and a kind smile were strength and sustenance for me. Why did they see the bum instead of the supplicant? Why did they see the drug addict, instead of the struggling man?

Then one cold, bitter December afternoon, I found myself shouting at a driver, then muttering to myself as he sped away. *How long have you been doing that, Ted?* I wondered, shocked by my anger. *How many minutes? Oh, Lord,* I thought, *how many days?*

I took a breath, calmed myself down, but I was still seething inside as I walked from car to car at the next red light, holding my same long sign. As usual, no one gave me money. No one rolled down their window or looked me in the eye. As I trudged back to my spot on the corner, grumbling angrily under my breath, a thought broke through my gloom: *They don't owe me. I'm not their responsibility. I am a sinner asking for a blessing. A blessing, not a reward.*

I thought of the woman with her five-dollar bill. I thought about her real gift: her belief in me. I thought about the twenty dollars I'd given Vic, and how wrong I'd been to seek money in return. There was no prize, I realized. There was no connection between morals and money. God didn't give you cash for doing good.

The thought came to me then: *You can't be asking, Ted. Blessing or reward, you can't be asking. You can only give.*

And what did I have to give? The same thing I'd always had. My Golden Voice. Was this what God had saved it for? Not for the radio, but for a kind word to the strangers who were always passing, passing, passing me by?

The light turned red. "Good morning!" I boomed to the first driver with a smile.

Nothing.

"God bless you, sir!" I boomed enthusiastically to the second driver, smiling even more. "Have a great day!"

Nothing again.

I walked the entire line without receiving a dime, but for the first time I didn't mind. *I'm asking for a blessing,* I told myself, *but my real purpose is to give.* I took that to heart, and I felt free: of entitlement, of anger, of the feeling of inadequacy for the journey ahead. There's no other way to say it: my heart opened. I felt gratitude—for life, for my tenuous sobriety, for Kathy, for Momma, for the strangers around me, and God above. I was on my corner to give back to the world as best I could—and every kind word said with an honest heart was my offering, and every penny I received was a blessing, a gift I didn't deserve.

Twenty minutes later, the driver of a pickup truck rolled down his window and growled, "Hey, buddy, you cold?"

Before I could answer, he threw a pair of beat-up gloves in my direction and sped off. I don't know if he was helping me or taunting me, but it was below freezing that morning and I was chilled to the bone. Those old gloves were like a gift from God. I slipped them on, looked to the sky, and said, "Thank you, Jesus."

Acknowledge Him.

Ten minutes later, someone rolled down their window and gave me a twenty.

"God bless you, sir."

In all your ways, *acknowledge Him.*

A few days later, a woman drove up and rolled down her window. "Good morning, ma'am. Have a wonderful day, and God bless you."

She handed me a dollar. "Thank you, sir," she said, wiping away tears. "I just needed to hear you say good morning today."

If I had a business, I'd tack that dollar bill to the wall. I'd point it out to all my customers, and I'd say, "My first dollar, right there. That's the first dollar of the rest of my life."

Because it's not the words that acknowledge Him, I realized in that moment. It's not the act. It's the reason you act. It's the feeling in your heart: the humility, the selflessness, the love. Most of all, it's the love.

Acknowledge Him.

In all your ways.

He will direct your path.

EPILOGUE

So that's the story of a black man's fall, then rise from the street to redemption. I won't say to success, because I'm still looking for ways to do good with my life. I was given an opportunity, and it's on me to keep working and make a difference. It's on me to keep saying, "Don't give up. Don't ever give up, because a miracle happened." A change came into my heart—that was the miracle—and if my broken addict's heart could change, then salvation is within anybody's grasp.

That's the important story, in my opinion. That's the story from the heart. But as you know, there's a little bit more. In early December 2010, as I was starting to understand God's golden message, a man named Doral Chenoweth took a video of me on my corner. My sign had attracted his attention, the one everyone told me to throw away because it was too long. Maybe my sign was too long for an advertisement, but that's never what it meant to me. The sign was my personal statement. I really did have a God-given gift of voice, and I was asking for help in using it.

Doral Chenoweth didn't post the video to the Internet until January 3, 2011, and by then I'd forgotten about him. Kathy and I had spent New Year's Eve depressed by our failures, but by New Year's Day, we were determined to finally enter rehab—separated, but still committed to each other—and make 2011 the year we beat the street. When the *Dave & Jimmy* show on local radio station WNCI called three days later, it was more than I ever imagined. And when the *Today* show wanted to fly me to New York?

Well, to say my life got crazy for a while, both exciting and scary, would be an understatement. My life exploded out of control. Twenty years of grinding homelessness in Ohio, and then only ten hours from my corner to a limousine in New York City, on my way to a $500-a-night hotel suite. I was riding with Kathy and my "management team" (my old friends Al Battle and Eric) on *Today*'s dime, and Kathy kept calling her sister Colleen from the car: "They have a driver! They have seats for ten! They have a bar . . . in the car!"

She called from the hotel room, too: "Bathrobes, really nice bathrobes! And . . . ohmygoodness, a telephone in the bathroom!"

The next morning, Doral Chenoweth's video of me standing on the corner, saying, "If you're listening to nothing but the best of oldies, you're listening to Magic 98.9," was showing on the marquee in Times Square. It was fifteen feet of Ted Williams's face . . . and another five feet of ratty hair.

I had a professional media escort to *Today*, where I sat down with Meredith Vieira and Matt Lauer. Fifteen minutes later, I was escorted off the stage and out a back door for a photo shoot, then an interview, then through another door to another set of cameras. Everyone wanted a piece of Ted Williams.

I wanted to see my momma. I had talked to her from the radio station in Columbus, but the next time I called, when we were boarding the airplane for New York City, a stranger answered and said, "This is a very good friend of your mother. Don't worry, she's safe." Then the woman hung up. Since then, nothing. I couldn't get an answer on her phone. NBC was pushing me in front of the cameras, everywhere I turned people were shouting, "We love you, Ted!" Al's phone was ringing off the hook, but I couldn't get in touch with Momma. I did Jimmy Fallon's show that night—it was fun, he gave me a new pair of shoes and let me say, "Coming up next, Jim Carrey"—but I was panicking inside. I'm from the projects, so I'm pessimistic. I figured some brothers thought I'd come into money, so they kidnapped my momma.

The next morning, six people, including a cameraman, met me at the door of my hotel room and ushered me into the elevator. "Turn left," they said at the bottom, then "turn right," and then, suddenly, I was walking into a conference room and Momma was sitting in a chair at the far end. I hadn't seen her in twenty years. We hadn't truly spoken as mother and son since my father died. The sight of her, ninety years old and beautiful, almost overwhelmed me. I started walking faster and faster, until I was almost running, muttering, "Momma, oh Momma, oh Momma." I knelt down and hugged her and the whole world heard what she whispered to me, because cameras were snapping and television stations were broadcasting the live feed.

"Don't let me down, son. Please don't let me down."

It was the same thing she'd been saying to me since I was a boy. "Please don't let me down."

"I won't, Momma. I promise, I won't."

The producers whisked me away. I was due on CBS's *The Early Show*, then it was over to ABC for a brief appearance with Robin Roberts. The other stations tried to prevent that one, but I loved Robin Roberts; there was no way I was turning down America's number one black anchor. Then it was uptown for voice-over work (and actual money) for Kraft Macaroni & Cheese—*You know you love it!*

By the time I got back to my hotel room, after eleven o'clock, I was exhausted. Al, Eric, and Kathy were celebrating in the room next door, but all I wanted was to collapse. It was too much. Too much. I undressed, ran a bath, and God help me, reached for the vodka bottle in the hotel mini-fridge. Then I turned on the radio, heard Hall & Oates's classic song "Kiss is on My List," and it just came over me, the reality that this was my life, it wasn't a dream, and I started dancing. I was standing in front of a floor-to-ceiling window overlooking Times Square, and I was dancing, buck naked, overcome with joy.

The next day, I flew to California and filmed *Extra* and *Entertainment Tonight*, and probably a few other shows I can't recall. I stood in front of one of those boards with sponsors' names all over it, just like a celebrity, and smiled for a hundred cameras. I was getting calls from DeGeneres, Seacrest, Trump, all the biggest names, but I committed to Dr. Phil because he flew two of my children, Julia and Desmond, to California. We took a limousine to Paramount Studios, Twentieth Century Fox, Madame Tussauds wax museum. We met Kobe Bryant! Can you believe that? We met Kobe! He signed my boy's shoes! That evening, after Desmond and Julia had gone back to the hotel, I took the limousine to the Hollywood sign. I stood on a hill overlooking the city, with the ocean sparkling in the distance, and yelled into the heavens, "I've made it! I'm Ted Williams, and I've made it!"

I hadn't made anything, of course. I hadn't done nothing but allowed myself to be swept into the fame game, and just like the first time, I lost my way. I started drinking that night, walked across the road to buy a forty-five-dollar bottle of Grey Goose vodka at the liquor store, because I'd always wanted to try the good stuff. The drinking was partly a celebration, partly to cover my nervousness and fear—but an alcoholic can't fall into the bottle, no good can come of that. And of course, my life started to fall apart the next day on Dr. Phil.

First, he grilled me about my criminal record and showed the world my mug shots. That didn't bother me, because I was used to humiliation. I'd made peace with that long ago. The *Dr. Phil* show was nothing but a busier street corner.

Then he brought out six of my kids. There was so much joy in the reunion, but also so much hurt and fear, so many unresolved issues, so many debts—and it was all so public. Before that week, none of us had ever been on television. Now we were on *national* television, with more than a million people watching. And the questions were personal, deeply personal. Sure enough, the show stirred painful memories, and emotions boiled over. Back at the hotel, I started drinking. My daughter Jenay (the one I made cry by smoking crack in the park, and whose heart was broken when I stood up Patty in 1996) got mad, I snapped back at her, and she hit me with an ice bucket. Next thing I knew, I was being questioned by the police.

Within twenty-four hours, I was being grilled again by Dr. Phil, who laid out all my failings for his national audience. That's when it started to hurt. That's when my mind turned dark, and I started to believe I wasn't someone America was pulling for, but a spectacle, another ill-suited "celebrity" the country was hoping to watch crash and burn. Newspapers started gloating over my criminal record like it was a revelation, even though I never denied my past. Howard Stern, one of my idols because he loved radio as much as I did, trashed me on the *Late Show with David Letterman*. *TMZ* reported I was hanging out with millionaires and eating at fancy Hollywood restaurants. That was bull. I was a long-term homeless man, and my stomach was torn up so bad I couldn't eat fancy food, even if I wanted to. Someone gave me a Subway sandwich, and my teeth were so sore I couldn't bite into it. I was still surviving, for the most part, on Wendy's chili.

That's when I should have reached out to God, like I did on the street corner. I should have asked Him to take me home. But I was in the middle of the storm, I was on national television, and Dr. Phil was offering rehab for my addictions. I didn't want to go. I wanted to be clean. I wanted to take advantage of this opportunity, but to confront me on national television? It unsettled my mind. The whole setup, I don't know, it didn't seem right.

I lasted twelve days in rehab. I know it was the addict in me that rebelled, but I blamed it on Dr. Phil. He kept putting me on the air—"Let's check in with homeless Ted!"—and it was so humiliating, I told myself that I had no choice but to call Al Battle and say, "Get me out of here." Al came to Texas, and we flew straight to California to rescue Kathy from her own rehab, which Dr. Phil had been kind enough to provide.

The newspapers said, "That's the end of Ted Williams." The Internet lit up with hate. Television commentators were saying, "I told you he wouldn't make it; I told you he was going back to the street!" like they were happy I failed, like they had won a dollar bet on whether a black man could make it in a white world like those dudes in *Trading Places.*

They were right . . . sort of. I moved into a sober-living house in California, where I tried to stay clean. I had new agents hired by Al Battle, good people, but I had no understanding of what they were pursuing or asking me to sign. They insisted I cut myself off from my past—for my own good, they said—but that meant turning my back on Kathy, and that's something I couldn't do. After all we'd been through, after all the times she stood beside me, I couldn't abandon Kathy to the street. She told Dr. Phil, "I'll go back to smoking crack and turning tricks for Ted." And she meant it. When he asked if that meant she'd die for me, she said, "I would."

I guess my answer, to my own surprise, would have been the same. I would have thrown it all away for Kathy. And I guess, in the end, you'd call that love.

In March, after three months in the public eye, I went home to Columbus. It wasn't working for me in California. I had people telling me what to do, but no friends. I had hangers-on, but no family. I'd given my first five thousand dollars to my children, but it didn't heal the wounds. I couldn't buy their love, not after what I'd done, and I didn't have enough money left to try.

Three months of fame, and I had no job. No home. No savings. No direction in life.

And no God. I'd lost sight of my spirituality in the whirlwind, and even worse, I'd lost my short-lived sobriety. I'd driven away from the sober house in Los Angeles one night, found a crack dealer in a tent city on skid row, and fallen back into the pipe. There was a moment, in Columbus, Ohio, in the spring of 2011, when I was one step away from being back on the street.

But I thought of my momma, and those heartfelt words: "Don't let me down."

I thought of my kids, and Patty, who'd never quite given up on me.

I thought of all the people inspired by my story, all the mothers and fathers who said I'd given them hope.

I remembered, especially, a church I'd visited the month before, in the middle of the publicity storm. I'd been invited to say a few words at a dinner banquet, but I was exhausted, overwhelmed, and

Al Battle wasn't even sure where we were supposed to go. By the time we were thirty minutes late, I wanted to turn back. I was sure it was a lost cause. Even when we were inside the building, we couldn't find the right place. Then Al opened a door—and suddenly, I was standing at the back of a crowded room. Oh, brother, was I nervous. I was quaking with fear. I'd been on television in front of five million people, I'd been exposed by Dr. Phil in front of a million more, but I was far more nervous in the back of that banquet hall.

"You're all right," Al said, putting a hand on my shoulder, but I didn't feel all right. I felt foolish. I felt unworthy. I felt . . . like I had nothing to say. I tried to creep to my table at the front of the room, hoping nobody would notice me. I got almost all the way there before the loud conversation around me turned into a low murmur, then slowly petered out. Someone handed me a microphone. I turned to look at the two hundred people behind me, with no idea what to tell them, and the first thing I saw was a simple gold cross hanging above the door.

"God is good," I said, without thinking. I heard a murmur from the crowd, people turning in their seats.

"God is good," I said again, raising my eyes to the roof. A few people clapped, and I felt my exhaustion start to ease. Someone said "amen," and then many voices said "amen," and I felt my doubt lifting, my soul rising up, and without a second thought I lifted one arm in the air and cried out from the heart in that melodious gift He had given me, "God is good! God is good!"

I started to cry. I'm not even sure what I was crying about, but I think it was joy and shame and thankfulness and the overwhelming power of salvation all wrapped into one. And as I cried, I could hear voices all around me shouting, "You're right, Brother Ted, you're right. God is good!"

I heard those echoes a month later, and I picked myself up. I let my old friend Al Battle go, who was well intentioned but in over his head, as well as my California agents. I stopped doing television appearances and interviews. I went back to church to renew my spirituality, along with my courage. I went to Kathy and said, "Remember how we talked about rehab at Christmas, right before the world turned upside down? Well, I'm going. I'm really going this time."

Then I went back to Dr. Phil, hat in hand, humility in heart, and asked for another chance.

He didn't want to take me back. My new attorney Bret Adams had to push and push to convince Dr. Phil of my sincerity, he had to make all kinds of promises, but in the end the doctor came through. After the craziness died down, after all the cameras had gone to chase some other lost soul, Dr. Phil offered me a second chance at rehabilitation. So say what you will about the man, and I know many people said he exploited me. I said as much myself at one time. But Dr. Phil saved my life. He paid for three months of serious locked-down rehab, and at the end of those three months, for the first time since I ruined my last chance at radio in 1996, I was clean.

I wasn't cured. No addict is ever cured. But for the first time in my life, I felt free.

Dr. Phil also put Kathy through rehab, and I would never have believed it a year ago, but she's clean now, too. I thought she was lost to the street forever, but she's taken off that tough skin, and she's opened her heart to the world. She's here with me now, on our little porch, in our little apartment, on the outskirts of Columbus, Ohio. She's drinking a cup of coffee, smoking a cigarette while I read the final pages of the book of my life. She has new teeth, courtesy of a dentist who accepted voice-over work instead of cash, and a cute dirty-blonde hairstyle, the work of her hairdresser sister,

Darla. She's also gained twenty pounds. She thinks she looks heavy, but she doesn't. She looks good.

"My sister Christine invited us over for dinner," she says, fiddling with her new phone.

"We don't have a car."

"She'll pick us up. We can stay the night."

"I'd like that," I say with a smile that shows off my own new teeth. I'm wearing new glasses (finally!) and a zebra-stripe bathrobe, and I'm staring out at a fake lake with a jogging path. The condo building where I'm renting is only one-fifth occupied and weeds are three feet high in the tennis courts, because there's apparently been a real estate crash, but I suppose the weeds will die off once the cold sets in, and the fountain in the middle of the lake will probably freeze, or maybe they turn it off in the winter, I don't know.

"I'm getting more coffee," I say—*from my own coffeemaker*, I want to add. I want also, for a moment, to kiss Kathy, maybe straight on the lips, but instead I pat her on the knee and walk to my own kitchen, with its own sandwich maker, and pour myself a cup.

I've made it, I want to yell. *I'm Ted Williams, and I've made it!*

But I don't, because I'm not fooling myself. Not this time. I've made it this far, but I still have a long way to go.

I'm an alcoholic and a drug addict, and I always will be, even though I'm sober now. But I have a sponsor. I have God. I have my meetings.

I have a family that cares for me, but who still doesn't trust me. My momma won't let Kathy into her apartment or even say her name out loud. My children keep their distance. All except Kaysha, the daughter conceived during my time at Friends of the Homeless. She never knew me, so I never broke her heart. She was sixteen when we met for the first time last year. She showed me a scrapbook. She'd been keeping pictures of every important event in her life: saxophone lessons, her first day of the school. On the front, it said "For my daddy."

I saw that and thought: I'm blessed. I have my second chance. I can give my daughter Kaysha what she's always wanted. I can support Kathy in her sobriety. I can keep setting a good example for my kids and grandkids until, one precious day, they accept me into their lives. I can talk to my momma with honesty, love, and an open heart, and God willing, I can finally make her proud.

I have voice-over contracts with Comcast and the New England Cable News, among others. I have commercials in the works. I still hear my voice every few days on Kraft advertisements saying *You know you love it*. I'm comfortable. I'm working. And I can see an even brighter future, maybe a regular radio show where I can be Ted Williams again, bring the listeners out of bed with energy in the morning, then ease them into the afternoon with songs for lovers. I'd like the opportunity to tell stories of second chances, maybe conduct inspirational interviews, but I can wait, I've got patience now. I can wait for the right opportunity to do good with my life.

I don't need fame because I have family and friends. I don't need more money because I already have so many good things. A clean bathrobe. A soft bed. A computer. A book. A toilet to sit on when I need private time. I don't have a kitchen table, but I have a balcony, a chair, a friend (Eric) who keeps me sober, and a woman who understands me, who would do anything for me, who loves me always and forever, even when I fail.

I have the God of my understanding, the God of my heart, so I don't need a million ears to hear my voice. I'm sure my publisher will want me on *Today*—and *Good Morning America*—and *The Early*

Show and *Entertainment Tonight* and Fallon and Kimmel and Letterman and all the other shows so interested in me the first time around. I'll love the experience, I admit, if it happens. I'll cherish it, because it will be an honor. But it's no longer my goal to shout my story to the world.

I'd rather stand with twenty-five people like you and speak it, because then I could shake your hand. I could give you a hug. I could let you see the real me, both the redemption and the pain, and I could tell you face-to-face, eye to eye, from my heart to yours: Keep the faith, brother. Keep the faith, sister. No matter what happens, keep the faith. Keep the love. Keep the hope. God is good.

God is good.

ACKNOWLEDGMENTS

To Momma: I can never thank you enough or make up for the pain I caused, but what I can do now is be the son you always wanted me to be.

To my father: We never saw eye to eye, but I know you wanted only the best for me.

To my children, Julia (my monkey), Jenay (my tutor), Tricia, Tangela (Doogie), Desmond (Dez-a-man), Tyrell (Tookie), and Kaysha: I love you with all my heart.

To Patty: You are special.

To Eric "Hardy-Bean" Harding: I would not be here today without you, my brother, my best friend, my sober-coach. And thanks also to Norma "Mama" Harding and the whole Harding family.

To Doral Chenoweth and *The Columbus Dispatch*: Thank you!

To the people who helped me in recovery: Dr. Phil, who kicked my butt on national television and gave me the reality check I needed; Ben Levenson and Rich Whitman at the Origins Recovery Center; and all the people I've met through NA and AA in Columbus, Ohio. You are truly my brothers and sisters.

To Bret Adams: What can I say about my "tough love" attorney, the only person who said no to me after I gained fame? You are my partner, my friend, my attorney, and I love you for what you have done for me. And to Cindy Smith, for her eternal patience.

To all my friends in the Kingsborough housing project in Brooklyn, New York, especially the Browns, the Ginns, the Halls, the Thompsons, and the Butlers. And a special shout-out to Lowell Williams and his entire family.

To all the people who helped me in the radio business, especially Doc Holliday at WVOE in North Carolina, Casey Jones at WVKO, and Rick Stevens at WCKX. To Jack Harris, the owner of the first black-owned-and-operated radio station in Columbus, WCKX, "Miracle 106." You were a pioneer and a visionary, and I'll never forget my eighteen months at #1 with you.

To all the people who were there for me after I lost my way, especially Al Battle, Rick Moore, Gary Chasin at Uncle Sam Pawn, Mark Henderson, Trina, and Melissa Killen.

To Kathy's sisters: Colleen Sariotis, Darla Pollina, and Christine Farley. You have been so important to us during this last phase of our lives.

To my book publishing team: My agents, Brandi Bowles and Peter McGuigan at Foundry Literary + Media; my cowriter, Bret Witter; my editor Megan Newman; and the rest of the amazing team at Gotham: Sophia Muthuraj, Bill Shinker, Susan Schwartz, LeeAnn Pemberton, Lisa Johnson, Lindsay Gordon, Laura Gianino, Ray Lundgren, and Sabrina Bowers. You are dream makers. Thank you for turning my life into a real book, one that will hopefully inspire and encourage people for years to come.

And finally, to Kathy: Thank you for sharing my journey, Tinky, and for being there through all the difficulties.

With God, all things are possible.

Amen.